Praise for *The Business of Heart*

"The Business of Heart is an inspirational road map for people to follow who want to make a difference in this country."

JENNIFER DUNN, *member of Congress*

"Some of the best work being done in communities today is being done by the remarkable heroes of this book. Here is a chance for every American to get to know them. More importantly, it is a chance to discover our own capacity to make a difference as social entrepreneurs or as their supporters. This is the only way to solve our social ills and make a great country even better."

GREGG PETERSMEYER, *senior vice president of Colin Powell's America's Promise and former director of the White House Office of National Service*

"We have a new group of superheroes in America who are waking us up to our responsibilities as citizens of this free land. This book not only tells the stories of these remarkable people, but it also outlines an approach for solving the problems in our communities. It is a must read for all Americans!"

NATALIE TAYLOR, *associate professor of management and innovation, Arthur M. Blank Center for Entrepreneurship, Babson College*

"Michael Glauser has captured the heart and soul of social entrepreneurs who sometimes single-handedly take action to solve our country's toughest problems. He has created a series of interesting vignettes that illustrate how these successful leaders are making a difference in their communities by helping people become self-sufficient. It is a must read for anyone who wants to contribute and give back to our country."

COURTNEY PRICE, *founder and CEO of the Entrepreneurial Education Foundation and Premier FastTrac International*

THE BUSINESS OF HEART

HOW EVERYDAY AMERICANS ARE CHANGING THE WORLD

MICHAEL J. GLAUSER

SHADOW MOUNTAIN

Library of Congress Cataloging-in-Publication Data

Glauser, Michael J.
   The business of heart : how everyday Americans are
changing the world / Michael J. Glauser.
      p.   cm.
   Includes bibliographical references and index.
   ISBN 1-57345-547-4
   1. Social responsibility of business 2. New business
enterprises. I. Title.
   HD60.G55   1999
   658.4'08—dc21   99-40424
                                                                              CIP

Printed in the United States of America   49510-6487

10   9   8   7   6   5   4   3   2   1

CONTENTS

CHAPTER · 1

SERVICE AS A WAY OF LIFE IN AMERICA

Henri Landwirth was taken to a concentration camp when he was thirteen years old. On numerous occasions he was supposed to die, but he didn't. His parents were not so fortunate. His father was killed when the war began; his mother, several months before it ended. After the war, Henri came to America with $20 in his pocket. He got a job in the hotel industry and worked his way up from night clerk to hotel owner. One day a "wish foundation" called and asked Henri if he would donate a room to the family of a child who was dying of cancer. Henri was delighted to help. The day the family was to arrive, Henri went to the hotel to meet the young girl. He was shocked to learn that Amy had died before making the trip—it had taken too long to arrange all the free services. That day, Henri made a promise he would keep: no more children would die in America before their last wish was fulfilled. With business savvy and remarkable passion, Henri rallied together a host of big-hearted corporations to provide funding, services and volunteers for his new organization. Today, Give Kids the World, in Orlando, Florida, fulfills the last wish of up to 7,000 children with terminal illnesses each year. For one full week, these special kids and their families stay in Henri's village, sleep in his villas, eat in his dining room, and visit all the theme parks of central Florida—for free! Henri is one of many social entrepreneurs who are serving our children.

Bill Strickland grew up in the inner city of Pittsburgh. He was going nowhere, fast. Getting shot, going to jail, and dropping out of school

1

were likely possibilities. Then one day he walked past the art room at his high school and saw a teacher making ceramics. He had never seen anything like it before. The teacher, Mr. Ross, agreed to show him how to make pottery. Bill soon discovered he was very good with clay. His self-esteem increased, he realized he had value, and he finished high school. During his freshman year of college, Bill created a "guild" to teach other inner-city kids about the arts. He wanted to replicate his own life-transforming experience with Mr. Ross. He wasn't interested in turning these kids into master craftsmen; he was interested in increasing their self-esteem and motivation. Bill's organization—the Manchester Craftsmen's Guild—grew from a small row house to a 62,000-square-foot facility. Today, all eleven schools in the Pittsburgh Public School System send kids to Bill's program. More than 400 students take courses in clay, photography, computer imaging, and jazz. Approximately 80 percent of these kids get into colleges around the country—very few programs match this success rate. Bill is one of many social entrepreneurs who are teaching our youth.

Susan Komen, a vibrant mother of two, was diagnosed with breast cancer when she was thirty-three years old. Her sister, **Nancy Brinker,** watched for three years as the ravages of cancer took Susan's life. At the time, breast cancer was a mystery—there were no comprehensive treatment programs and no support groups, but there was tremendous physical and emotional suffering. The two sisters grew weary of waiting for hours in uncomfortable chairs in drab treatment rooms. Susan used to say, "When I get well, Nanny, will you help me do something about this?" Nancy would always say, "Of course I will." When Susan died, Nancy did not wallow in endless despair or rage blindly at the injustice of the world. Instead, she quietly set out to fulfill her promise to Susan. She started off in the guest room of her home in Dallas with $200 and a shoebox full of friends' names. Her first fund-raiser—a women's outdoor polo tournament—was rained out. As she stood on the field crying, with color running down her hands from the soggy crepe-paper streamers, she felt she had failed. From that humble beginning, Nancy went on to build the nation's largest private funder of breast cancer research and education—the Susan G. Komen Breast Cancer Foundation. The organization now raises $50 million a year to help prevent breast cancer. Nancy is one of many social entrepreneurs who are healing our afflicted.

Bea Gaddy was a welfare mom in Baltimore. She struggled for years to feed herself and her children. One day she decided to do something about it. She borrowed a garbage can on wheels from her pastor, wheeled it to several local grocery stores, and asked for any day-old food they might be throwing out. As she wheeled the can back to her apartment, all the neighbors peered out their windows, wondering what she was doing. Since Bea knew some of them were hungry too, she invited them over to share her newfound food. This was the birth of Bea Gaddy Family Centers. On Thanksgiving day that year she served thirty-nine people dinner in her backyard. The next year she served 600 people. Today, Bea has multiple locations that serve Thanksgiving dinner to 45,000 people and provide food and other services to 80,000 more throughout the year. Bea is one of many social entrepreneurs who are feeding our hungry.

Ranya Kelly needed a box to mail a gift, so she went behind the shoe store at her local strip mall. When she looked in the dumpster, she discovered 500 pairs of shoes. She couldn't understand why a company would throw away perfectly good shoes when so many people needed them. She loaded the shoes into her car, took them home, and cleaned them up. They had been marked with yellow spray paint but were otherwise in good condition. Ranya took the shoes to a local shelter in Denver run by the Catholic Church. When she got there, she noticed a pregnant woman without shoes. The priest told Ranya they didn't have any shoes to fit the woman. This was the beginning of a lifetime quest to collect shoes and other articles for the needy. Though her organization is called The Redistribution Center, Ranya is affectionately known as "The Shoe Lady." Since her first trip to the shoe store, she has donated 600,000 pairs of shoes to schools, shelters, hospitals, Indian reservations, police departments, and fire departments. Ranya is one of many social entrepreneurs who are aiding our needy.

AMERICA'S NEW HEROES

Entrepreneurship is exploding in America. More than a million new businesses are being formed each year, and the number continues to grow. Many factors are fueling this entrepreneurial revolution. One obvious catalyst is technology. Computers have affected every household, business, and industry. As powerful communication systems continue to become smaller and more affordable, more of us computer-ize, cellular-ize, and Internet-ize our lives. Companies of any size now have access to the same powerful technology once available only to our largest corporations. In addition, we can now work anywhere we want: at home, in a car, on an airplane, in a hotel room. Technology has aided the recent boom of home-based businesses in America.

Another force feeding the frenzy of entrepreneurial activity is the globalization of our economy. For decades, we did business in a fishbowl in America. Now the playing field is the ocean. Companies from all over the world are dumping products into our economy at lower prices than we can produce them here. Escalating competition has set corporate America into a tailspin. Our mammoth bureaucracies are scaling back growth, cutting costs, and reducing their workforces. The downsizing of America has put thousands of astute executives and managers out on the streets. Many of these individuals are seeking to establish their independence by starting their own companies.

Within this entrepreneurial explosion is a new American hero—the social entrepreneur. Social entrepreneurs create organizations to solve America's toughest problems: hunger, poverty, housing, healthcare, education. These are people with heart, people with passion, people with principle, people who want to make our world better. When all is said and done, they would rather make a difference than a pile of money. They are much more than idealistic do-gooders, however. The nonprofit world is full of benevolent people who lack leadership skills—they erroneously believe their organizations will succeed because their cause is good. Consequently, the failure rate is high in this work. In contrast, successful social entrepreneurs have the complete package: extraordinary compassion *and* organizational savvy. They know how to seize opportunities, build powerful teams, and get the most out of limited resources. Most important, they figure out how to generate revenue to keep their dreams alive.

Who are these social entrepreneurs and why do they start their remarkable organizations? In my book *Glorious Accidents,* I summarize three years of research I conducted on America's top entrepreneurs. One of my more intriguing findings was how these people got into business. While knocking around some industry, they discovered an unmet need, received hoorays from a credible mentor, then seized the opportunity with passion. Very few of them planned on starting a business until they first discovered the need. I observed this same pattern with the social entrepreneurs I interviewed during the past year. While going about their lives, they stumbled onto an overwhelming need, developed real compassion for the sufferers, then took action to alleviate the problem. No one I interviewed quit a job and sat around saying, "I want to start a nonprofit organization; what should it be?" Instead, they saw the need first, felt the compassion, and then took the action.

This pattern—See It, Feel It, Do It—seems to be the impetus for launching a social organization. You'll see it over and over in the stories that follow. Harry Granader, for example, visited children's hospitals while he was building a Ronald McDonald House. He was extremely touched by the kids he met with cancer, heart disease, and kidney disorders. He started Camp Mak-A-Dream to free these children from the challenges of their diseases. Meredith Blake was abused as a youth. While in law school she met others who had experienced this same tragedy. She started Break the Cycle to stem the spread of domestic violence in America. Trevor Armbrister went to Midland, Texas, to write a story for Reader's Digest about a volunteer organization. He was overwhelmed when 3,000 people showed up and repaired the homes of 100 elderly and handicapped individuals. He returned to Washington, D.C., and started his own service organization—Christmas in April.

My purpose in sharing the stories of these incredible social entrepreneurs is threefold. First, I want to promote service as a way of life in America. I hope to illuminate needs, stir hearts, and stimulate action. If we never see the suffering, we'll never feel the compassion; if we never feel the compassion, we'll never join hands to solve our problems. Second, I want to introduce you to these marvelous American heroes. These are the role models we should be talking about in our homes, schools, and religious organizations. If we don't document great lives, they will be lost to future generations. Third, I want to summarize the keys to starting and building a successful nonprofit organization. If you discover you have the passion and skills, you too can create a thriving social venture or at least support the worthy endeavors of those who do.

Let's begin by discussing our obligation to serve each other as a way of life in America. To fully understand our responsibilities, we need to look to our past, know where we have come from, and apply the principles that have made this country great to the challenges of today.

WE THE PEOPLE

America is a grand experiment in freedom. No loftier document has ever been written about a people's desire for self-government than the Declaration of Independence. It boldly proclaims that all people have certain unalienable rights that cannot be taken from them, and that government exists to protect these rights. One of these sacred privileges, the pursuit of happiness, was a new political doctrine at the time. This was not a call for self-centered hedonism but a cry for all citizens to work together for the good of society. The document ends with a commitment from the people to make the grand experiment work: "For the support of this Declaration, with a firm reliance on the protection of divine Providence, we mutually pledge to each other our Lives, our Fortunes and our sacred Honor."

As the Declaration was circulated, its majestic language sent the hearts of the American people soaring. Conditions could not have been better for the experiment in self-government to take hold: the colonists were aflame with passion, committed to one another, and facing a common enemy. It's not too surprising that this little band of freedom lovers was able to take on the British Empire and win.

It wasn't until after the Revolutionary War, during times of peace, that the grand experiment faced its first real test. As magnificent as the Declaration was, it clearly was not complete. The states needed to enforce common laws, circulate currency, regulate trade among themselves, and negotiate with other governments—yet they were acting like independent countries. The Constitution of the United States was an attempt to "form a more perfect union" among the people. It established a stronger national government, clarified the relationships among the states, and further defined the rights and liberties of every individual. Such an elaborate document detailing how a free people would solve their own problems was previously unheard of.

With all the pieces in place, our forebears were ready to prove to the world that self-government would work. They were all in the grand experiment together, forging new frontiers and new concepts in living. They understood the importance of participation from every individual. They worked together to build each other's barns and plant and harvest each other's crops; they held town meetings to plan their schools, roads and cities; they cared for the sick and afflicted and adopted the children of those who had tragically passed away. It was a marvelous display of "all for one and one for all."

Eyes from abroad watched the experiment with great interest and curiosity. The ruling nobles were sure it would fail; the common citizens hoped it would prevail and set a precedent for the world. In 1831, Alexis de Tocqueville, a French political philosopher, came to America to examine the experiment in self-rule up close. He published his observations in a multivolume work entitled *Democracy in America*. Tocqueville quickly noticed that the essence of this new society took place in its small communities. After spending time in a New England township he recorded:

> When an American needs the assistance of his fellows, it is very rare for that to be refused, and I have often seen it given spontaneously and eagerly. When there is an accident on the public road, people hurry from all sides to help the victim. When some unexpected disaster strikes a family, a thousand strangers willingly open their purses, and small but very numerous gifts relieve their distress. It often happens in the most civilized countries of the world that a man in misfortune is almost as isolated in the crowd as a savage in the woods. That is hardly ever seen in the United States.

Tocqueville reported having seen this phenomenon within various professions in Europe, but not within society at large. People of the same profession, he argued, were "liable to the same ills" and, consequently, willing to help their peers in times of need. In other words, they were in the same "professional boat" and willing to work together to keep it from sinking. On a much broader scale, the citizens of this new experiment were all in the same "human boat" and willing to do everything necessary to keep it afloat. According to Tocqueville, this intense commitment to succeed came from the opportunity to participate in the process and influence the direction of society. Through this ability to solve their own problems, these early Americans enjoyed tremendous social cohesion and a common political psychology—it was almost a civil religion. As optimistic as Tocqueville was about some aspects of American society, however, he predicted the experiment would fail, largely because of the issue of slavery, which was inconsistent with the overall philosophy of a free society.

True to Tocqueville's prediction, the grand experiment faced its fiercest trail during the Civil War. The Northern States believed that the rights described in the Declaration and Constitution applied to all human beings, and that states could not withdraw from the Union. The Southern States believed that slavery was necessary to preserve their way of life, and they felt they could leave the Union anytime they chose. It was the most unusual war in history; it wasn't fought for power or money, for land or possessions; it was fought to determine if every individual who lived on American soil would enjoy the same liberties. The two sides had a similar vision but different manifestations of the dream.

The Civil War reached its climax on the battlefield of Gettysburg. After two years of brutal fighting, the Southern army had depleted its resources and badly needed a major victory if it was to have any chance of winning the war. Robert E. Lee's bold strategy was to march into Northern territory, draw the Union army away from Washington, deliver a crushing blow, and open the way for the capture of Washington and other Northern cities. His Southern army of more than 70,000 men was intercepted by the Union Army of 90,000 men in the small borough of Gettysburg, Pennsylvania. For three days, fellow Americans engaged in the most significant battle in the history of the United States.

I recently visited the National Military Park at Gettysburg. In the visitors center I saw the faces and read the names of men on both sides of the conflict who paid the ultimate price defending their version of the dream. I was intrigued by the story of an unidentified Union soldier killed in battle and found clasping a picture of three children to his breast. A civilian from Gettysburg passed the photo on to a Dr. Bournes of Philadelphia, who circulated copies to newspapers throughout the North in an attempt to identify the children's father. The soldier was identified by his wife as Orderly Sergeant Amos Humiston of New York. Dr. Bournes went to Portville, New York, to return the original picture to Mrs. Humiston. The experience triggered a major fund-raising effort to build a home for the orphans of deceased Union soldiers. Consistent with Tocqueville's observations, the community saw a pressing need, felt true compassion, and worked together to solve the problem.

Outside on the battlefield, I climbed Cemetery Ridge and envisioned the melee of battle unfolding before me. I heard the tumultuous thunder of artillery on the ridge, belching canisters of death over the struggle below, sending men and horses and weapons into the air, and leaving smoking craters in the earth. I saw the Union soldiers march across the wheat field in crisp columns like shimmering wheat in the sun, only to be harvested by the guns of the confederate reapers hidden in the woods. I envisioned the hand-to-hand combat of the frenzied forces, surging and retreating, not knowing from moment to moment who was the victor and who was the vanquished. I pictured the wounded soldiers scattered across the peach orchard—some in blue, some in gray—writhing in agony in the hot July sun, begging for relief—too many to be attended to by the short supply of medics—then quietly, thankfully crossing the threshold of mortality, all for the sake of the grand American experiment in freedom.

Especially touching was my ascent up the boulder-strewn hill, Little Round Top, where Colonel Joshua Chamberlain and the 20th Maine held the left flank of the Union line. Chamberlain had been a professor of rhetoric and modern languages at Bowdoin College before the war and was unskilled in the strategy of battle. He was told to "hold this ground at all costs." If he failed, the Confederates could flank the line and surround the Union Army. After staving off numerous Confederate charges and running out of ammunition, Chamberlain, in desperation, ordered a bayonet charge down the hill. The shrill cries and unflinching attack of his crazed soldiers drove off the Confederate forces for good. According to Chamberlain, his men would have charged all the way to Richmond if he had not called off their fury. As his little band of 200 marched back up the hill, rounding up Confederate soldiers, they discovered they had taken more than 400 prisoners—a ratio of two to one. Did Chamberlain understand that his spur-of-the-moment bayonet charge may have won the battle, and even the war for the Union? Good thing he didn't know much about soldiering. When I asked an attendant in the visitor's center for literature about Joshua Chamberlain, she smiled and said, "Nobody ever talked about him until after the movie *Gettysburg.*" Here was an exceedingly brave man whose heroic deeds nearly slipped through the cracks of American history until his story was told. In that same spirit, I want to make sure the heroic acts of the community servants featured in this book do not fall by the wayside.

After three long days of treacherous warfare, Lee finally retreated his battered army back to Virginia. More than 43,000 troops were dead, wounded, or missing—23,000 from the North and 20,000 from the South—every one of them Americans. After two years of consistent Southern victories, the image of Southern invincibility was shattered. When Lee crossed the Potomac, he knew in his heart the war was over. The South would never again have the troop strength to mount a major offensive against the North.

Before leaving Gettysburg, I visited the site of Lincoln's renowned address, which he delivered four months after the battle on November 19, 1863. My mother tells me we are related to Lincoln in some distant way, so we affectionately refer to him as "Cousin Abe" at our home. It was almost a fluke that Lincoln spoke at the battlefield that day. The organizers originally invited three revered poets to the event—Longfellow, Whittier, and Bryant—but all three declined for various reasons. Not to worry; Edward Everett, president of Harvard University and one of the greatest orators of the time, was available. He could hold the masses in thrall, but he needed two months to prepare his two-hour speech, which he delivered from memory. Lincoln was casually asked through his bodyguard to give a few remarks at the end of the program, only because he had made it known that he planned to be present.

Lincoln's three-minute remarks were one-fourth as long as the opening prayer offered by Reverend Stockton. Yet his 272 words "refounded" America. Lincoln's focus was the preservation of self-government, not the carnage of the battle. The war was simply testing whether a government of the people could sustain the proposition of equality over time. In a sense, Lincoln revolutionized the Revolution by clarifying the imperfections of the Founders' achievements. His succinct words told us how to interpret the Declaration of Independence and clarified aspects of the Constitution without altering either document. Most important, to ensure that those who died at Gettysburg did not do so in vain, he challenged the living to increase their dedication to the unfinished business of making equality in self-government work. A government of the people, by the people, and for the people must survive, not just for America's sake but also for the benefit of the world. Those who heard Lincoln's majestic message walked away with a new interpretation of the past and a clearer vision of the future. Though the war would continue for another year and a half, the grand experiment in freedom had survived!

TODAY'S CHALLENGES

Our grand design in freedom is being tested again today, ever so subtly. Our nation is much larger, society is more complex, and we are being bombarded with more information than ever before in our history. And yet in the midst of this information explosion, many of us are lonely and isolated. During the founding of our country, people worked together to build their barns, mend their fences, and harvest their crops. This reliance on each other for physical labor produced a strong emotional bond between these early citizens. Now that we no longer need each other's physical assistance, we have also forfeited the emotional bonds it once created. We can live next door to our neighbors for years and never get to know them or understand their problems. The truth is, millions of Americans are hungry, millions live in poverty, and a shockingly high percentage of our citizens live below acceptable literacy levels. Our basic support unit, the family, is deteriorating, domestic violence is widespread, teenage pregnancy is rampant, children are growing up without strong role models, drug use is on the rise, and gang membership is increasing.

Unfortunately, along with the growth and increasing complexity of society, we've delegated many of our problems to the government. Since we all pay a substantial amount of taxes, and we elect public officials to represent us, it's natural to assume that the government should solve our problems. If only it were that simple. Most of us now recognize that government cannot and should not be expected to solve all of our challenges. Our toughest social problems are simply too vast, too complex, and too expensive for government to render effective and efficient solutions. Alongside government, private enterprise is chipping away at some of our social ills. While many companies are making contributions in health care, housing, and education, business by its very nature can work only on problems that produce a return on the investment made. Like government, private enterprise is only a partial solution.

Ultimately, the solution to our problems is the same as it has always been: "We the People." We need to resuscitate the "township" spirit observed by Tocqueville. We need to recover our tradition of a single society working for the good of all. We need to reclaim for ourselves the role in public life we have forfeited to the government through our own inaction. I'm not advocating a nostalgic return to

frontier days. Throughout my career, I have been a strong propo-
nent of change. People change, products change, organizations
change, societies changes—and we need to change with them. But
rather than simply accommodate change, we need to initiate it so
we can control the direction it takes. What I'm suggesting is that we
look to our past to understand where we have come from, take the
sound principles upon which our country was founded, and integrate them into our modern world to solve our social ills and make
a great country even better.

Actually, I believe that most Americans are willing to assist the
needy and work to benefit society. It's what noble hearts aspire to
do and willing hands work to achieve. In his autobiography, the dis-
tinguished humanitarian Albert Schweitzer made this observation
about human nature:

> Judging by what I have learned about men and women, I am
> convinced that far more idealistic aspiration exists than is ever
> evident. Just as the rivers we see are much less numerous than
> the underground streams, so the idealism that is visible is
> minor compared to what men and women carry in their
> hearts, unreleased or scarcely released. Mankind is waiting and
> longing for those who can accomplish the task of untying
> what is knotted and bringing the underground waters to the
> surface.

So why don't more of us get involved in community service if
it is in our hearts to do so? I think there are several reasons. First,
we don't believe that one person can make much difference.
Nothing is further from the truth. Chamberlain and Lincoln each
made small contributions that changed the world, and we can do
the same. Starting off small is the only way to begin anything big.
It's like trying to move a mountain with nothing but a shovel. You
look up at the massive mound, then down at your little shovel, and
you say, "There is no way." But you want to help, so you start shov-
eling anyway. Before long, others see your example and decide to
join you. Soon you have ten shovelers, then a hundred, then a

thousand—and the mountain gets moved. You'll see this phenomenon over and over in the stories that follow. One person's passion
ignites a flame in a host of others, and serious problems get solved.

Another reason we fail to take action is because no one asks us
to help. Studies show that volunteers often join a cause just because
someone asked them to. For all who would like to contribute but
haven't been asked, consider this book your call to action. Everyone
in America needs to pick up a shovel, choose a mountain, and
become part of the effort for change. Without significant contributions from all of us, our social problems will never be resolved. But
if we join together in concerted effort—the government, private
enterprise, and we, the people—there isn't a problem in America we
cannot solve. Tremendous power is unleashed when all sectors of
society work together toward common objectives. After the battle of
Gettysburg, Joshua Chamberlain penned the following words about
the power of collective action:

> The inspiration of a noble cause involving human interests
> wide and far, enables men to do things they did not dream
> themselves capable of before, and which they were not capa-
> ble of alone. The consciousness of belonging, vitally, to some-
> thing beyond individuality; of being part of a personality that
> reaches we know not where, in space and time, greatens the
> heart to the limit of the soul's ideal, and builds out the
> supreme of character.

The time has come to create a new American culture where giving of ourselves is a rite of passage, an important part of becoming
a full-fledged member of society. All of us must participate and
teach our children to do the same. Call it a tithe, call it an offering,
call it dues for the privilege of living here. Part of this new culture
will include making those who valiantly exercise their civic responsibilities our new American heroes. And as we have done in the past,
we can set a standard for the world with our new model of civic

engagement. Let's recommit ourselves to making the grand experiment in self-rule and citizen problem-solving work—once again!

MAKING A LASTING DIFFERENCE

Stephen Covey, author of *The 7 Habits of Highly Effective People,* is fond of the saying, "Give a man a fish and you feed him for a day; teach him how to fish and you feed him for a lifetime." I try to practice this philosophy with my children—and they are sick of it! When Eric asks, "Dad, will you get me a bowl of cereal?" I reply, "Get a boy a bowl of cereal and you feed him for a day; teach him how to pour his own cereal and you feed him for a lifetime." When Tyler begs, "Pops, will you look up Spencer's number in the phone book for me?" I answer, "Look up a phone number for a boy and you find him a friend for a day; teach him how to look up phone numbers himself and you find him friends for a lifetime." When Marc asks, "Father, will you edit my report?" I respond, "Edit a boy's report and you get him an 'A' for a day; teach him how to edit his own reports and you get him 'A's' for a lifetime." They've heard this so much they now cringe before they ask. But I tell them, "If I drop dead tomorrow, you've got to be able to take care of yourselves."

I believe that this philosophy is critical to solving the social ills in our country. Unfortunately, our two-party system often becomes polarized at opposite ends of the helping continuum. Those on the left see themselves as the party of compassion and view those on the right as greedy egotists. Those on the right see themselves as the party of responsibility and view those on the left as bleeding-heart liberals. Actually, both parties have honorable intentions; they simply focus on different stages of the helping process. If we take care of immediate needs only and don't teach responsibility and independence, we don't solve anything permanently. In fact, addressing only immediate needs can perpetuate and expand problems, as is the case with some government programs. On the other hand, trying to teach independence to people who are hungry, naked, and ill will have little impact until their immediate needs are met. If people are hungry, we need to feed them; if people are naked, we need to clothe them; if people are sick, we need to heal them. Then we must move to the next stage of teaching people how to take care of themselves; otherwise, those we are trying to serve will be hungry, naked, and sick again tomorrow.

During my career, I have counseled many people who have experienced unemployment, financial setbacks, poverty, and emotional distress. It is always easier to give them food, clothing, or money than it is to devise permanent solutions to their problems. Making a lasting impact requires developing real compassion for these individuals and then spending hours in face-to-face interaction, teaching them the principles required to turn their lives around. This always involves conveying new information, new attitudes, and new behaviors: better grooming, work habits, budgeting, career skills, and so on. I have found that immediate assistance is always more effective when given as part of a broader, life-altering plan. This is the hard work of service—it's the difference that makes a difference. In his seminal book *Revolution of the Heart,* Billy Shore describes the importance of personal involvement in producing lasting change:

> No amount of money can substitute for personal involvement. That's not to say that social programs don't have costs and need financing. They do. But the essential ingredients are not dollars, grants, stipends, or government contracts. The essential ingredients are people who are willing to go to neighborhoods not their own, to work with people not like them, and to share the strengths and skills and attitudes that have enabled them to be successful in their own lives.

No one I interviewed has perfected this model better than Mimi Silbert, the founder of Delancey Street. Her organization is patterned after the extended immigrant family whose members arrive in America and work together to achieve their dreams. The members of Mimi's family, however, are drug addicts, ex-convicts, and homeless people—the underclass of society. Upon entering Mimi's program, participants first learn about themselves: how they ended up where they are, what attitudes they have developed along the way, and what changes they need to make to succeed. They also learn basic maintenance skills, such as how to take a shower, how to wash clothes, how to set a table, and how to cook healthy meals. Next, they complete the equivalent of a high-school education. Finally, they learn three different career skills by working in actual businesses Delancey Street owns and operates. After four years in this exceptional family, participants reenter society as productive citizens. More than 90 percent of these people never return to drugs or jail—a success rate unheard of in the helping professions.

Other social entrepreneurs in this book also champion comprehensive models of change. Most of the organizations you'll read about meet immediate needs *and* provide long-term solutions to tough problems. For example, Best Buddies International provides friendship to the mentally retarded, but it also helps them finish school, find jobs, and live independently. Bea Gaddy's organization feeds the hungry, but it also teaches them about self-worth and how to succeed in careers. Break the Cycle offers legal assistance to those suffering from domestic violence, but it also helps people get out and stay out of abusive relationships. First Book gives at-risk children their own first book, but it also provides mentors who help these kids learn to read and excel in school. Athletes Against Drugs teaches young people to stay off illicit drugs, but it also teaches them about leadership, teamwork, and community service. This list goes on and on.

To solve America's challenges, we need to follow the examples of these social entrepreneurs and create models that address the entire process of change—models that effectively move people from point A to point B. For these programs to work, they must be rich in both compassion and long-term vision. The first step is to realize that we are all in this experiment together, and that differences between us are superficial compared to the countless ways we are alike. When we see children who are suffering, we need to see our own children; when we meet people who are experiencing pain, we need to see ourselves; when we encounter human beings in dire circumstances, we need to see souls with great possibilities. The next step is to help those we serve become strong enough to stand on their own. The ultimate goal is to help them become givers themselves who use their newfound knowledge and skills to lift and enlighten others. This completes the cycle of service and starts another iteration. Hopefully, the process will continue to expand until it fills the nation with charitable activity.

THE MIRACLES OF GIVING

Giving produces three outcomes that border on the miraculous: (1) it redeems the receiver, (2) it transforms the giver, and (3) it renews the community. The benefits to the receiver are obvious. Thanks to Food From the 'Hood, kids who were going nowhere are now going to college. Thanks to the Adolescent Employment Readiness Center, adolescents with chronic illnesses and physical disabilities are finding employment and becoming independent. Thanks to Christmas in April, the elderly across America are receiving the assistance they need to make their homes safer and more comfortable. Thanks to Athletes Against Drugs, young people vulnerable to drug use are committing to stay drug free for life. And thanks to the Children's Miracle Network, hospitals across the country are receiving the equipment and support they need to better heal our children.

Even more fundamental than the assistance provided is the life-altering transformation many receivers experience when served by organizations with both compassion and long-term vision. Many of those we seek to help—the hungry, the poor, the criminals, the homeless, the addicts, the abused—need a whole new orientation to themselves and to life. As Mimi Silbert explains, it's like taking people from a foreign country and trying to integrate them into America. To be successful, these strangers to society need a total makeover in cultural values, behavioral norms, and life attitudes. Fortunately, when shown genuine compassion and taught essential life skills, most people are malleable enough to make life-altering changes. Hence, we see the homeless earn college degrees, addicts free themselves of their vices, the needy become self-sufficient, and ex-criminals successfully integrate themselves into society. These people are miraculously redeemed from lives of failure by our heroic givers.

Equally profound is the impact of giving on the giver. Simply put, caring about others to the point of taking action significantly improves the quality of one's life. When A helps B, A benefits; when B helps C, B benefits; when C helps D, C benefits. It's a natural law recognized by most world religions. In Christianity it's called the Law of the Harvest: we reap what we sow. In various Eastern religions it's called the Law of Karma: present actions determine future destinies. In the vernacular of the street, we say, "What goes around comes around." The fact is, every action produces an equal reaction, not necessarily similar in kind but always equal in magnitude and effect. Whether we intend it or not, our actions set up a chain reaction of events that eventually come back to us. Hence, evil begets evil, good begets good, mercy begets mercy—it all adds up! Those who serve others establish a stream of positive consequences that bless their own lives.

In his intriguing book *The Halo Effect,* John Raynolds, president of the National Peace Garden Foundation, documents the unplanned side effects of volunteering. People who regularly serve others make new friends, develop new skills, enhance their leadership abilities, increase their professional contacts, do better in their careers, and enjoy greater physical and emotional health. Some of these by-products will eventually come to all givers, unless we serve only to get them. Ironically, hidden agendas and personal motives erase the rewards of service. When we give "this" expecting to get "that," we will always be disappointed: people will fail to thank us, we won't get the recognition we desire, someone else will win the election, and so on. Service rewards the giver only when it is selfless, which means the "self" is not involved. When we give unconditionally, we enjoy the peace of helping others without having to keep score, worry about fairness, or evaluate the value of our investment—and therein lies the reward.

By far the most significant miracle of giving is the overall improvement in life satisfaction enjoyed by the giver—something we all desire. One of the fastest-growing epidemics in America is depression. Mental health professionals fear we are entering an age of melancholy as more and more people experience this disease at younger ages. Approximately eighteen million Americans suffer from depression at any given time, and about three and a half million of these are children. One out of five people will struggle with this illness over a lifetime. The World Health Organization now ranks depression as the number-one disabling disease for women, and number four overall. The cost of treating this illness, including lost work time, now exceeds $40 billion annually.

While the causes of depression are complex, experts agree that feelings of alienation may be one factor contributing to the unraveling of America's emotions. In former times, we enjoyed tight-knit families, extended family ties, and stronger links to our community—everyone belonged to something larger than themselves. Today, children are having children, divorce is rampant, single-parent homes are commonplace, dysfunctional families are on the rise, and we have fewer links to our extended family and community. Many people feel isolated and alone in a world full of people, which is disheartening and overwhelming.

Success rates for various treatments of depression have not been impressive. The most common approaches are drug therapy, psychotherapy, or some combination of the two. Unfortunately, about 30 percent of those who take antidepressants receive no relief, others receive only partial relief, and many relapse into severe depression while still taking the medication. The results of traditional psychotherapy are equally underwhelming. Spending months rummaging through someone's past may pinpoint the cause of despair, but it doesn't always make the person feel better. In fact, excessive attention to the past may exacerbate the tendency to "get stuck" in negative ruminations that explain and perpetuate the illness. More effective are the forward-looking, short-term strategies that teach people to think differently about themselves and the world around them.

As a volunteer counselor to people with emotional challenges, I have discovered that serving others is a tremendous therapy for depression. Focusing on the needs of others gets us outside of ourselves and reconnects us to the human family. It nullifies our natural tendencies toward self-absorption, gives our negative ruminations a rest, and helps us see that life is not that bad after all. As we continue to focus on others as our priority, our own burdens—real and imagined—become lighter and easier to bear, and they may even go away. I am not an expert in the field of mental health, and I'm not suggesting that giving is the panacea for all emotional ills. In fact, I always encourage people to attack their emotional troubles from all possible angles: medication, therapy, exercise, nutrition, *and* giving to others. But my own observation is that serving the less fortunate is a powerful inoculation against depression and a strong antidote for those who have the disease.

Milton Erickson, an icon in the field of short-term therapy, tells a story that illustrates the power of service as a natural antidepressant. A friend of his had an aunt in Milwaukee who was despondent. She was fifty-two years old, independently wealthy, had never married, lived alone, and had no friends. She read the Bible every day and attended the Episcopalian Church religiously, but she would slip out at the end of the service, never speaking to anyone. Milton agreed to visit the woman on his next trip to Milwaukee. When he got to her home, he noticed three large African violets in full bloom in her sunroom. He knew that African violets, though beautiful, are delicate plants that quickly die if neglected. After seeing the violets, he told the woman he had some medical instructions that would help her get better if she followed them exactly. She passively agreed to do whatever he asked.

Erickson told the woman to go to a nursery and buy African violets of all different hues, 200 gift flowerpots, and some potting soil. He told her to grow as many mature African violets as she could and to take good care of them. Then she was to give an African violet to every couple that got married in her church, every family that had a baby, everyone that got sick, and every family that experienced a death. He also told her to donate African violets to every bazaar held at the church. Erickson believed that anyone who took care of 200 African violets would be too busy to be depressed. His premonition was correct. The woman became known as the "African Violet Queen of Milwaukee" and had many friends of all ages. She died in her seventies having been happy and productive for more than twenty years. The incredible change took place after just one visit from Erickson, with no probing into the woman's past or insight about her personality. She simply found a worthwhile cause to occupy her attention and link her again to the human family.

The joy of service is so powerful that many organizations, originally created to meet a need in the community, are now becoming havens for life transformation. The Human Service Alliance (HSA) in Winston-Salem, North Carolina, is a marvelous example. HSA is an all-volunteer organization that cares for the terminally ill during their last few months of life. All volunteers are of equal status and do all the jobs required to maintain the operation: cooking, cleaning, washing clothes, taking out the garbage, and changing bedpans—no job is below anyone. Doctors, teachers, lawyers, and carpenters work together to help the guests enjoy their remaining days in mortality. The cost of caring for the terminally ill at HSA is one-twentieth the cost of a hospital—and it's free to the patients. The experience in raw human existence connects the volunteers to the dying, to their own mortality, and to humanity in general. People from all over the world come to this special place looking for themselves and discover the healing balm of selfless service.

And so it is that giving miraculously transforms the giver. When we are totally absorbed in ourselves, we experience a full range of emotions: anger, fear, depression, anxiety. When we focus our attention on others, the primary emotion we cultivate is love. As we continue to serve, expecting nothing in return, our capacity to love will grow to include many individuals, regardless of their circumstances. Almost magically, service leads to love, and love liberates. It frees us from our own problems and helps us discover our true value as members of humankind. Such is the fate of those who give with the pure motive of helping people in need.

Finally, the third outcome of service that borders on miraculous is the impact on the community. Obviously, giving can benefit all communities, at least indirectly. If people are stronger and better connected, our problems get solved and our cities become better places to live. In the stories that follow, you'll see how the efforts of Linda Kantor totally changed a neighborhood. Linda first built a housing complex for Latino elderly in New Haven, Connecticut. Next, to clean up the surrounding area, she built a home across the street where the old and young could congregate. Her plan was to have the Latino elderly teach their art, culture, and skills to the youth in the community in after-school programs. Courses are now offered in music, cooking, sewing, jewelry-making, and other employable skills. Today, a neighborhood once plagued with drugs, shootings, and destruction is being transformed into a place where people walk the streets, talk to one another, and participate in community projects. As Linda explains, "It seems to be spreading down the street, person by person, house by house. People who haven't talked to each other in twenty years are now working together." Hence, when service becomes a way of life, everybody wins: the receiver, the giver, and the community.

OUR SOCIAL ENTREPRENEURS

A lot of people in America are doing remarkable things. The social entrepreneurs featured in this book are but a small sample of the many modern-day heroes who are changing our world. My objective was to include a variety of people from across America—male and female, black and white, young and old—who are working on a variety of social problems: hunger, poverty, illiteracy, addictions, abuse, health care, and education. While some social entrepreneurs are doing marvelous things with animals, the environment, and legislation, I limited my focus to people who are working directly with people.

I also tried to select role models who have proven their staying power. The organizations you'll read about have stabilized beyond the hand-to-mouth stage, which means they have creatively addressed their funding problems. I purposely avoided organizations that rely exclusively on state and federal money—such entities are merely extensions of the government. While a few of our social entrepreneurs receive government support, it is not their primary source of revenue. Most have created unique fund-raising events and effective partnerships with businesses. The best organizations generate revenue from their own products and services—they are essentially nonprofit businesses that create profit to support their cause.

I discovered these extraordinary people in newspapers, magazines, and books, on the Internet and from referrals. After creating my "wish list," I sent each person a letter explaining the project;

everyone I contacted agreed to participate. Next, I conducted and recorded detailed interviews and transcribed the tapes. For the most part, the stories contain the actual words these people delivered to me. I edited the manuscripts only to clarify chronology, eliminate redundancy, and improve overall readability. I wanted you, the reader, to have the same experience I had meeting these heroes, hearing their dialogue, feeling their energy, and sensing their compassion.

As you read the stories, notice how many of these social entrepreneurs give the gifts they have acquired from their own experiences. Having "been there" enhances both compassion for the sufferers and understanding of the solutions. For example, Henri Landwirth knows what it's like to face death every day. He is the perfect one to comfort America's dying children. Crystal Davis knows what it's like to go without food and shelter while growing up. She is perfectly positioned to help the needy. Nancy Brinker knows what it's like to have breast cancer in her family. She is well suited to attack this problem. Bill Halamandaris knows what it's like to lack the resources required to go to college. He is the perfect person to help disadvantaged kids get an education.

Like these social entrepreneurs, we can best contribute by giving the gifts we've been given. We are always more effective when we draw from our own heartfelt experiences. Have you overcome depression? Pass this gift on! Have you learned about job hunting? Pass this gift on! Have you defeated a serious illness? Pass this gift on! Have you developed a talent in the arts? Pass this gift on! Humanity is blessed by humanity. If we fail to share the gifts we've been given, they'll have no lasting value.

I hope these stories will motivate you to adopt service as a way of life. All the organizations you will read about need helping hands. If you are touched by one of these causes, get involved. Contact information can be found at the end of the book. Even more important, we need to duplicate these organizations across America. Every city needs a Christmas in April. Every high school and college campus needs a Best Buddies. Every community needs a Break the Cycle. Every city needs a Community Hope Center. And every state needs a Delancey Street.

If you have problems in your community that are not addressed by these organizations, you may feel impressed to launch your own service enterprise. The final chapter of this book outlines the keys to starting and building a successful nonprofit organization. The concepts presented were gleaned from my interviews with our talented social entrepreneurs.

So here we go. Prepare yourself to be touched by these unusual heroes with heart. You'll love their zeal, smile at their quirks, and revere their compassion. If we follow the example of these service superstars, we can have a huge impact on society. Let's make the grand experiment in freedom work!

CHAPTER · 2

SERVING OUR CHILDREN

*Suffer the little children to come unto me, and forbid them not:
for of such is the kingdom of God.*

MARK 10:14

*We can wait for a world revolution while we avert our eyes from
the sight of hungry children on our subways, outside our malls,
in our neighborhood parks; or we can answer the call for a revolution of the heart simply to see another possibility.*

GLORIA NAYLOR

The soul is healed by being with children.

FYODOR DOSTOEVSKY

It's a chilly North Dakota December—just two weeks before Christmas.
Eleven-year old Alvaro Garza and his two buddies are frolicking home
from school along the frozen Red River when one spies a dead squirrel
lying on the ice. As the three step out for a closer look, the thin ice
crumbles under Alvaro's feet. His helpless friends watch in shock as he
disappears into the bone-chilling, black water.

At 4:30 P.M. in the winter dusk, rescue workers troll the ice-choked
waters with pike poles, hoping to find Alvaro's body before dark.
Suddenly worker Darryl Hendricksen's pole snags something—it's
Alvaro, limp and lifeless. He has been submerged for an hour and ten

minutes; his body temperature is seventy-seven degrees. Hendricksen's heart sinks; he knows that only a miracle will save this boy.

But a miracle is waiting for Alvaro when he reaches St. Luke's emergency room—a miracle heart bypass machine that warms his blood one degree every five minutes. The machine has been purchased only the year before with funds raised for the hospital by the Children's Miracle Network Telethon. Before having this machine, the hospital would have sent Alvaro to Minneapolis, a trip he never would have survived.

At 6:00 P.M., Alvaro's heart begins to beat about twenty times a minute for the first time in almost two hours. The next day his temperature is back to normal and he responds to his name. By Christmas, he is home with his family. The following June in Disneyland, a healthy, exuberant Alvaro stands on the stage at the Children's Miracle Network Telethon, representing many children the world over who are alive today because of this amazing organization.

Many children in America are having a rough go of life. The decline in moral standards, the heightened divorce rate, and the dissolution of family ties are creating challenges that were less formidable in previous decades. Here are some of the facts we are facing today.

Over 50 percent of high-school girls in America, ages fifteen to nineteen, have had sexual relations with one or more partners; 24 percent have had experiences with three or more partners. Nearly a million girls in this age group become pregnant each year; 350,000 of these are seventeen or under. Consequently, thousands of babies in America are being born into less than favorable circumstances. Overall, one out of three children is born to an unmarried woman, and approximately 30 percent of all children under the age of eighteen are being raised in single-parent homes. Obviously, single parenthood is not the cause of America's woes. A child raised in a loving single-parent home is far better off than a child born in an abusive and neglectful two-parent home. But single parenthood does place additional economic and child-rearing strains on both parent and children.

Poverty is also a growing challenge for America's children. Of the thirty-six million people who are considered hungry or food insecure, more than fourteen million or 40 percent are children. This represents approximately 20 percent of all the children in this country, which is the highest child poverty rate of any industrialized nation. Every day in America, twenty-seven children die from the effects of poverty, and 800 poor women give birth to high-risk babies with dangerously low birth weights. Poor kids are not only vulnerable to a variety of diseases related to malnutrition, but they also have a difficult time accessing even the simplest medical care, such as preventative immunizations. An example is the 57 percent increase in hospitalization rates since 1980 of children under five years of age who suffer from asthma—a relatively easy illness to diagnose and treat.

In addition to illnesses related to poverty, 9,000 children are diagnosed with cancer each year. Behind accidents, cancer is the chief cause of death in children under fifteen years of age. Nearly 2,000 children die each year from the disease. While the number of cases is relatively small, the suffering experienced by these kids and their families is enormous. The children are usually homebound; healthy siblings often feel neglected; finances are seriously taxed; and marriages undergo severe strain. These families need real support to survive the crisis.

Here are a handful of heroes who are working to improve the plight of America's children. Henri Landwirth created his revered organization, Give Kids the World, to offer hope and joy to children with terminal illnesses. Eleven-year-old Aubyn Burnside started Suitcases For Kids to make moving a more pleasant experience for children in foster care. Mick Shannon and his partner Joe Lake launched the Children's Miracle Network to raise funds for children's hospitals across America. Peter Gold and Kyle Zimmer created First Book to help underprivileged children cultivate reading skills. And Harry Granader and his wife, Sylvia, started Camp Mak-A-Dream to give children suffering with cancer some good times to help them through the bad times. These social entrepreneurs have tremendous compassion for children in difficult circumstances. You're going to love their stories.

HENRI LANDWIRTH

Henri Landwirth is an icon in the nonprofit world. His renowned organization, Give Kids the World, was only a dream a dozen years ago. With incredible passion, business savvy, and the support of dozens of corporate partners and thousands of volunteers, Henri has built a model organization. Give Kids the World is currently fulfilling the last wish of up to 7,000 terminally ill children each year. Here is Henri's story:

I was born in Belgium, then moved to Poland with my family at an early age. When I was thirteen, we were taken to concentration camps because we were Jewish. Over the next five years, I experienced five different camps, one of them being Auschwitz in Poland. I was really supposed to die—that was the ultimate objective—but I was young and very strong, so I was always put to work.

My father was killed early on. He was marched to a mass grave and made to stand in a hole with several other men. A German soldier stood behind him, pointed a rifle at the back of his head, and pulled the trigger. He was murdered without cause and buried in an unmarked grave. My mother lived nearly five years. A few months before the war was over, they put her on a boat with 1,000 other female prisoners and exploded the boat at sea. They were all killed except for a Polish girl who was an Olympic swimmer; she was able to get to the shore somehow. I contacted her later, and she remembered my mother.

The most difficult thing about the camps was the hunger and

thirst I had to live with daily. It's difficult to explain hunger unless you experience it yourself. You think about food constantly and become like an animal. Some prisoners were so hungry they ate the infected food of those who died of typhoid, just for the sake of feeling full for once. I did this myself one time and became very ill. I was taken to the hospital, something the guards only did when a prisoner was dying. When I woke up the next morning, everyone was dead but me, so they sent me back to the camp.

Toward the end of the war, we were taken out of the prison and marched outside of town. I understood German and knew the guards had been ordered to shoot us. I was surprised at the depth to which I did not care; I just couldn't take it anymore. The other prisoners also seemed pleased that the end was here. When we got to the forest, one of the soldiers turned to his comrades and said, "The war is almost over. I don't want to kill these people." The other soldiers shrugged their shoulders; they didn't seem to want to kill us either. Then the soldier said to me, "Line up over there facing the trees. When I raise my gun, run into the woods."

I ran for about half a mile, then started walking. For the next few weeks, I wandered from village to village, trying to stay hidden. I would steal food whenever I could. I estimated I wandered for several hundred miles. One day I found an empty house on the outskirts of a small town and went inside and fell asleep. I was awakened by an old woman who told me I was in Czechoslovakia and the war was over.

The next few years were very difficult. With all the things that had happened in the camps, I felt like I was living on borrowed time. I had a big need to do something my parents would be proud of, but I only had a sixth-grade education. I had missed all the important things a young person should experience between the ages of thirteen and eighteen. I went back to Belgium for a while but couldn't make it there. Many times I slept through breakfast because there was nothing to eat—it was that bad! I was alone, discouraged, and wanted to leave Europe because the memories were too diffi-cult. So in 1950 I came to the United States with $20 in my pocket.

After being here three months, I was drafted into the army—this was during the Korean War. At first I thought it was a joke, but the United States has the right to draft you when you apply for your first citizenship papers. Actually, I wanted to be a good citizen and didn't mind being a soldier. I felt that to be an American, you had to fight for this country. The problem was I didn't understand English well enough to even take commands, never mind go to war. This was a tremendous fear to me.

I went for basic training, then received orders to go to Korea. Here again, another miracle took place. At the eleventh hour, my name was called, and I went to see a captain. He said, "I understand you are a diamond cutter. We would like you to stay in this country and get involved in our crystal cutting." I had learned diamond cut-ting in Belgium, so I went along with him. Crystals had to be cut and placed in the radios to make them work. At the time, I didn't know there was no connection between diamond cutting and crys-tal cutting. Once they discovered this, I ended up cleaning windows in the radio shop.

After I got out of the army, I used the GI Bill to enroll in the New York Hotel Technology School. At the same time, I got a job at the Wellington Hotel. I wanted to prove I could succeed in this great country, so I tried to do everything with tremendous passion. I started doing all the different jobs in the hotel. I worked the night desk, was a cashier, a room clerk, and so on. I was hungry like a sponge to learn as much as I could. The most important thing I learned is that the hotel business is a people business. If you want to succeed, you have to succeed with people. To succeed with peo-ple, you have to give them what they want. The best way to do this is to listen, not talk.

In 1954, I married an Italian girl. The Italian custom is to give money to the people getting married. We received $800 and went to

Miami on our honeymoon. Since we were starting a new life together, we decided to stay in Florida. Before long, I was back in the hotel business because I knew all the jobs. I worked my way up from job to job until I was managing hotels. I managed three hotels in Cocoa Beach during the heyday of the space program—that's when I met all the astronauts. Then I managed five Holiday Inns in Florida. When Disney announced they were coming to Orlando in 1969, I got the Holiday Inn franchise with John Glenn, who had become a very good friend of mine. He and I opened four hotels together and have been partners for over thirty years.

In 1986, we donated several rooms to a "wish" foundation that was bringing a young child and her family to Orlando. The girl had incurable cancer, and her one wish was to meet Mickey Mouse. Just before the family arrived, the general manager of our hotel came to my office and said, "We just got a cancellation on the rooms we were giving away to the terminally ill child and her family." I said, "Why did they cancel? Did they go someplace else?" He said, "No, I understand the child died because it took so long to make all the arrangements." I looked at him and said, "This cannot be. How can we not fulfill a child's last wish in America?" I was very disturbed by this and began looking into how the wish foundations worked. I discovered it took so long because they were trying to arrange for all these free services. They were calling airlines, hotels, rental car companies, and so on. Some companies would help and some would not. By the time they got the tickets, rooms, and transportation, six to eight weeks would pass. I also learned that 75 percent of terminally ill children want to see Mickey Mouse as their last wish.

I decided to do something about this problem and started Give Kids the World that very year. I wanted to be able to bring kids here from anywhere in the country almost overnight. I converted a storage room at the Holiday Inn into an office and staffed it with one secretary and a telephone. We began to build our dream with a hundred square feet and a commitment that no more children would die before their last wish was fulfilled.

The first thing I did was visit every theme park in central Florida and ask for their help. Every one of them was extremely receptive—Disney, Sea World, Universal Studios. They promised me all the tickets and everything I needed to make this happen. I then contacted other companies that could help: hotels, rental car agencies, and so on. Eighty-seven hotels in Orlando agreed to join our efforts. Next, I needed some volunteers to go to the airport and meet the children. I had built a facility for a group of elderly people called the 39ers, so I called their executive director. He said, "There is no way these people will ever respond to your request; they are in wheelchairs and on oxygen; they won't go to the airport!" I said, "Just let me talk to them." I got about sixty of them in a room, and when I finished, fifty of them signed up! [Laughs.] They said, "Yes, that's exactly what we want to do. We want to be the grandparents who go to the airport and greet these children." We now have between 150 and 200 volunteers working at the airport each week.

During that first year I organized an advisory board to help find corporate sponsors. Equitable Insurance Company gave us our first donation. I went to New York to receive their check for $75,000. As I left their office, I looked across the street at the Wellington Hotel where I had worked for $42 a week just a few years before. I had to laugh. It could only happen in America. A person can come here without any money, without any English, and can become whatever he wants to become. Everything is possible in this wonderful, wonderful country of ours. In my wildest dreams I never expected I would do as well as I have, both professionally and financially. I have a tremendous love for this country.

Our first year we had 380 families come. The second year, we served more than 700 families. The year after that, more than 1,200 families came. As our numbers grew, it became more and more difficult to get hotel rooms at certain times of the year. I finally decided we needed our own village to accommodate the families. We started with sixteen villas on sixteen acres, then quickly jumped to thirty-two villas. Holiday Inn adopted us as their charity and loaned us $1 million to get started, which I have since paid back. I also borrowed $700,000 from a bank in order to finish the village quickly. The rest of our support came from builders, contractors, landscapers, plumbers, electricians, and hundreds of people who generously donated money, materials, and labor. It was really amazing how excited people were to help.

We have continued to grow each year. Right now we have ninety-six villas on fifty acres. About 350 wish foundations send us children. They find the kids and put them on a plane, and we fulfill their wishes. We never turn down a child. We can now serve 7,000 families a year. We have had children here from all fifty states and from fifty countries. They stay for one week with their whole family, completely free! There is no way they can spend any money here. And all the children, including siblings, are treated the same way. There is no difference between the children who are sick and the children who are healthy. The brothers and sisters of sick children often suffer too, because they don't get the attention they need.

Our biggest concentration in the village is the children; we don't think about grownups at all. We have a dining room where they eat breakfast and dinner at small tables and chairs. The villas have large bedrooms and bathrooms, and everything is wheelchair accessible. Even the pool has a ramp that wheelchairs can go in. The Disney characters come twice a week, and Universal and Sea World send their characters—they are very much a part of everything we do. We have a fishing pond for the kids, a new theater, and a train station.

During the week, the families go to all of the theme parks. When they come back, every child gets a gift every single day. One night during the week, the parents go out to dinner by themselves. Some of them have not done this for years and years. We bring in very qualified people to entertain the kids while they are gone. Some of the parents come back early because they don't know what to talk about or how to behave. They also like the village so much they often prefer to stay here. Some families choose to stay in the village all week long. One family came here and went to all the parks; then a few months later we saw them again. I said, "What are you doing back here?" It was very embarrassing because the mother said, "Well, I have two children that are terminally ill, so we are back. But this time we want to stay right here in the village all week. We don't want to go anywhere else."

The funding for our operation comes from many wonderful corporate sponsors. Disney, Universal, Sea World, Proctor & Gamble, and K-Mart have been big supporters over the years. Coca-Cola got on board a year ago, and NASCAR is with us right now. Our sponsors love what we do for the children and are excited to help us. They do great things for us financially and otherwise. The amazing thing about these relationships is that everything is done on a handshake. We are dealing with some of the biggest corporations in America and have nothing in writing. This is very unusual. These companies also work together in some fashion, so we bridge their efforts. Here is a funny thing you may want to know. Hard Rock has a presence in our village because they gave us money to build a train station. Planet Hollywood is right next door because they gave us money for a theater. Now these two companies are competing minute-to-minute in the business world. When each chairman came to me, I told him about his competitor's interest in the village. I was amazed when they both told me the same thing: "Henri, when it comes to dying children, all this competitive stuff is out of the way. We don't care about being next to each other." It's so wonderful to work together in that spirit.

We also have more than 2,000 volunteers that make our program work. Volunteerism is the foundation of Give Kids the World. Every time a family comes in, a greeter meets them at the gate and takes them through the airport. Some of these families have never traveled with their sick children before. At the village, we have meal servers, groundskeepers, gift givers, transporters, and entertainers. We have fifty schools that come into the village at Christmastime and decorate the villas for the children. The school kids raise the money, buy the trees and decorations, and try to make each villa as spectacular as possible. Things like this happen here every day.

Our corporate partners are also a great source of volunteers. Disney, for example, continues to provide more support each year. They help in every aspect of village operations, from babysitting to landscaping. They have also taken on a number of special projects. Each of their hotels has adopted one of our buildings, and their employees provide maintenance, painting, repairs, and general upkeep. At Christmastime, their volunteers turn the village into a winter wonderland for children. Over the years, Disney has provided hundreds of thousands of dollars of services. Whenever we need something, they always say yes. One time we had a little girl here who loved Snow White. When Snow White visited the village, this little girl was beside herself with joy. When she later succumbed to her illness, her family contacted me. The wanted to use Snow White on the child's tombstone and needed help in gaining permission. Our friends at Disney gave it, and the child was buried with a Snow White marker on her grave.

On general terms, we know for a fact we extend the lives of some of these children. They don't all die; some go into remission and live to be healthy grownups. On one occasion we had a request to bring a family down immediately because the little girl was dying—the doctor had given her two or three days to live. Coming here was her last wish. When they were on the plane, the child put her head on her mother's shoulder and started to breathe very strangely. The mother truly felt that her child was dying. When they arrived at the village, the mother went to register, and the child opened the car door and started running around. The mother went into hysterics because she didn't know what was going on. She quickly called the doctor. He said, "Just let her run as much as she wants; don't stop her." Apparently, the child got so excited to see the beautiful surroundings of the village that something happened to her. She lived for another six months!

This work has completely changed me. My life now has new meaning. I feel wonderful getting up each morning knowing I am making a difference in this world. It's such a wonderful feeling that I believe it's a gift from God. The problem is, I found out about it at the late age of sixty. I would encourage younger people to become givers earlier in life. It's the way to find peace and happiness. No question! My children are all involved in charity work, which pleases me tremendously. I always tell them, "I started too late; maybe you can make up for it." [Laughs.]

> You have to truly believe in what you are doing, then do it for the right reason. If you have a hidden agenda people will see through that.

Success for a nonprofit organization is not that complicated. There are two things you really have to keep in mind. Number one, you have to truly believe in what you are doing, then do it for the right reason. If you have a hidden agenda— you want to be a senator or congressman or whatever—people will see through that. So do the right thing for the right reason, then concentrate on your mission. Focus on what is best for the organization, not for you. Many charities start off with the best intentions; then egos get in the way and people forget their mission. The funny thing is, if you start politicking for power, you lose it immediately.

The second thing is, you have to run a charity like a business. It *is* a business! You have to have passion for what you are doing, but you also have to understand finances, marketing, managing people, and building strong partnerships. Lots of people work with their hearts, which is wonderful, but they think things will work out because they are giving. Not so! You have to build an effective organization and develop funding sources to continue your work.

It's ironic, but growing up in concentration camps really had a positive impact on me. Many of the survivors got sour and ended up in crazy houses because they couldn't forgive the Germans; their hate destroyed them. Other people, like me, have forgiven them and done something with their lives. We have the urge to be the best we can because we know life is so short. I know what it's like to be waiting to die. This has had a big impact on what I am doing here. I see a definite connection between me and the children. They have no control over their lives, and I had no control over my life in the camps. They are skinny and pale, and I see myself in their faces. This has really drawn me to them. I just want to devote my life to serving these families. My daughter sent me a beautiful quotation by Winston Churchill that summarizes my feelings. It says, "We make a living by what we get, but we make a life by what we give." I inscribed that in a mosaic in a prominent place in the village. That's what my life is about today.

AUBYN BURNSIDE

Aubyn Burnside is the founder of Suitcases For Kids, a worldwide organization that collects used suitcases for children in foster care. She started the organization when she was eleven years old. Aubyn has been featured in newspapers and magazines nationwide. She has appeared on the Oprah Winfrey Show and in a campaign that aired during Monday Night Football and the NBA Championships. In 1998 she was named a National Honoree of the Spirit of Community Award by Prudential Insurance and the National Association of Secondary School Principals. Aubyn has personally collected more than 17,000 suitcases for children in foster care. Here is her story:

My older sister Leslie went to work with foster children a couple of years ago. One night just before Christmas, she accompanied a social worker and a uniformed policeman as they took four children into foster care. The children were very upset, but the mother didn't even care! Leslie was horrified when the children stuffed their belongings into garbage bags. She said, "Where are the suitcases for these children?" She found out that foster kids usually don't have suitcases. Leslie told our family about the situation, and I was shocked! I thought, "Those children must feel like garbage." Leslie asked my mother to donate our unused suitcases from the attic; she thought at least a few children could be helped.

In November of 1996, I decided to do something. I was eleven years old at the time. My family travels a lot, so I know what it's like to pack clothes. I also know what it's like to have a nice suitcase. I wanted these foster kids to have a suitcase of their own so they would feel special. I thought it might give them some dignity and self-respect. Thinking that people might receive new luggage for Christmas, I decided to wait until after the holidays to begin my project. I thought it would take me a year to get 300 suitcases, one for every child in foster care in my county.

I named my project Suitcases For Kids and appointed my younger brother Welland, age seven, the junior chairman. I printed flyers and put them all over Catawba county in libraries, museums, and grocery stores. Then I asked Sunday schools, 4-H kids, Girl Scouts, and Boy Scouts to help. I also asked churches to put the information in their bulletins. People could call if they wanted me to pick up their suitcases, or they could take them directly to social services.

I waited two or three weeks after distributing the flyers, and nothing happened. So my mom and I bought some suitcases at yard sales and the Salvation Army. Then, surprise! Suitcases started pouring in! Everybody started calling, wanting to donate their unused suitcases. One lady had just given hers away, so she purchased seven at a resale shop. A prayer group went to the Goodwill store and bought everything they had—it was thirty-one suitcases! My priest's godmother even mailed me suitcases from 100 miles away. In only seven weeks, I met my initial goal of 300 suitcases.

Our first delivery was really exciting. It was in March of 1997.

My 4-H friends and I took 307 suitcases to the Catawba County Department of Social Services. The newspaper and television station were there, and the social workers came out and clapped and thanked us for meeting a long-standing need. Some of them even cried, they were so happy.

Then in April I was invited to speak in Burlington, North Carolina, at a social-services convention. I decided to create a handout so the delegates would know how to contact me if someone wanted to start the program in their area. It actually turned into a twelve-page starter kit that contained a history of the project, easy steps for getting started, commonly asked questions, press releases, reminders, and a thank you letter.

After the meeting, people started calling and asking for starter kits. Scouts, 4-H groups, churches, and community groups all wanted to collect suitcases in their counties. Then requests started coming in from neighboring states. Meanwhile, suitcases kept rolling in! So Welland, my friends, and I kept collecting and cleaning them. We delivered them to counties farther and farther away. People really caught the spirit of the project.

Before long, Suitcases For Kids was spreading across the nation like wildfire. In September of 1997, *National Geographic WORLD* and Pizza Hut inducted me into the Kids' Hall of Fame. A producer from the Oprah Winfrey show read the article about me in *WORLD* and invited me to appear as a guest. I was pretty surprised. When I got there they said, "*You're* Aubyn?" I said, "Yeah." That's all I said because I was pretty scared. I was afraid they were going to say, "We're sorry, but we don't have enough time, so we're clipping your part of the show." [Laughs.] I think they were afraid I wouldn't come through for them. But Oprah named me a Young Angel in her Angel Network. After that, people wrote to the show to get my address, and I sent hundreds of free starter kits all over the country.

So lots of volunteers of all ages have joined Suitcases For Kids. I have mailed out more than 2,300 starter kits. The program is active in all 100 counties in North Carolina, all fifty states, and in seven foreign countries. In addition, suitcases have been donated to medical teams traveling to Mexico, Bolivia, Chile, and other places around the world. These teams have to carry their medicines with them, so they use our suitcases. Then they leave them there for storage.

Thousands and thousands of suitcases have been collected in the past few years. My goal is to train people to automatically recycle them to children in foster care. I've personally collected around 17,000 so far. A 4-H group in Smith County, Texas, collected 1,000 in a month. A Boston travel agent discounts tours if you bring in your used suitcases. Airline personnel donate their suitcases when they are issued new ones. A Girl Scout in California is putting a notice in every restaurant in her town. And a Boy Scout in Richmond, Virginia, started the project in memory of his Scoutmaster who was a foster parent. I have received many letters from grateful foster children over the past few years.

> My project shows that any person of any age can volunteer.

Suitcases For Kids now has funding from Families for Kids, a program sponsored by the W. K. Kellogg Foundation to place foster children in permanent homes within a year. JC Penney has also supported the project through the Golden Rule Award. *Seventeen Magazine* and Cover Girl cosmetics are additional corporate sponsors. We use the money we receive to print and mail out the free starter kits.

My project shows that any person of any age can volunteer. It makes me feel especially good knowing I'm helping children who really need us. I met a fourteen-year-old boy in foster care when I was delivering suitcases to the Burke County Department of Social Services. He was on his way to his seventh foster home. I told him to pick out whatever suitcases he wanted. He selected a big sports duffel bag and a huge suitcase. He told me they were the best presents he had ever received. Just remembering that boy is a constant motivation to keep Suitcases For Kids going. Foster kids tend to get lost because they don't get much news coverage. I want to make people aware of their needs—not just for suitcases but also for loving families. Lots of foster children have been adopted because our project has received so much attention. That's pretty exciting!

MICK SHANNON

Mick Shannon and his partner Joe Lake are the founders of the Children's Miracle Network, an organization that raises $200 million a year for children's hospitals across America. The organization's success is a miracle itself. Starting off with nothing more than a dream, Mick and Joe traveled across America for three years setting up an elaborate network of television stations, children's hospitals, and corporate sponsors. Today, the Children's Miracle Network produces the largest television fund-raiser in the world. Brandon Tartikoff, the former president of NBC Entertainment, referred to the telethon as "the finest live television show produced." Here's the story:

Right out of college, I went to work for the March of Dimes in Boise, Idaho. Five years later, I moved to the March of Dimes in Salt Lake City. At the time, the Utah organization was doing a local telethon with KSL, one of the best stations in the market. It was raising about $300,000 a year, most of which was going to Primary Children's Hospital. When I took over, I thought the show seemed a little stale, so I made some pretty dramatic changes. I moved it to the Salt Palace, found some new stars, got new production people, and made it more contemporary and exciting.

After that first show, I carefully studied the tape; being young and naive, I thought it looked pretty good. I got my team together and said, "Guys, this is great live television. We ought to do this for the whole country." It seemed silly to put forth all that effort for a small market like Utah. I concluded that we could produce a national show with the same amount of effort and resources.

So we prepared a presentation for the parent organization, the March of Dimes in New York. They said, "Yeah, we like this, but you'll have to move to L.A. to make it work." That's not what we had in mind at all. We were confident that we could do it from Utah. At the same time, it was clear that all the money raised should go to the local children's hospital in each area. The March of Dimes was leaving 40 percent in the local community and taking 60 percent back to New York. This is when I started thinking about creating a new organization. Working for the March of Dimes was a great experience; it taught me a lot about community-based fund-raising. But I really felt there was a more effective and efficient way to do things.

I talked to my friend and colleague Joe Lake about my idea, and he was quite enthusiastic. Fortunately, he was at a point in his career where he wanted a new challenge. Joe is the greatest salesman in the world. He has no fear. He'll literally pick up the phone and call the White House. We make a good team because we both think that anything can be done. Joe and I talked to our families about the sacrifice this thing would require, and everyone was supportive. So in 1982 we launched the Children's Miracle Network—that was the name from the beginning.

Early on, our thinking was influenced heavily by our relationship with KSL and Primary Children's Hospital. They are both great organizations. We thought, "Wow! What would it be like to partner with a Primary and a KSL in every community?" Our vision was to find television stations in each community that would carry the telethon, children's hospitals in each area that would receive the funds, and corporate sponsors that would provide the support necessary to get us started. We quickly adopted three guiding principles: First, 100 percent of monies donated from any area of the country would remain with the local children's hospital in that market. Second, the show would be produced at a much lower cost than other telethons. And third, it would all be done with dignity and class—we had no intention of exploiting sick children.

We literally started out in Joe's basement with nothing more than a card table and our dream. Then we got a bank to donate some office space. We went down to the state surplus warehouse in Salt Lake City and picked up some desks and chairs. They were heavy! I remember because our office was upstairs. [Laughs.] I put the phones in my name because we didn't have any credit. But we knew that phone calls would not be enough. After all, who had ever heard of Mick and Joe? So we went to the airlines and begged for free tickets—Republic and Western agreed to help. Then we told Marriott what we were doing, and they gave us free hotel rooms. Without these commitments we wouldn't have survived a very shaky beginning.

The first thing we did was visit different cities to sign up the television stations and children's hospitals. Since I knew everyone in Boise and had a good reputation there, that was our first stop—it was a fairly easy visit. But we knew we couldn't be successful staying in the Boises of the world—corporate America wouldn't buy into that—so our next trip was to L.A. Our thinking was, "If we're going to do this, why mess around?"

We met with a guy named Chuck Velona at KHJ in Los Angeles. Chuck starts saying, "The last thing we need—" And we interrupt him with, "Yeah, we know, the last thing this country needs is another telethon, but we're here to convince you that this is not just another telethon. This effort can help 250,000 kids every year. It can improve the quality of their lives and even save their lives. And everyone who shows up will be helped regardless of their ability to pay, twenty-four hours a day, 365 days a year. This is a critical situation right here in your own community. You don't need to look very far to see where your resources will be used." Well, Chuck leans back and he's sweatin' a little by now. He rubs his old bald head and says, "I really don't want to do this." And we said, "We know you don't, but let's go over to the children's hospital so you can meet some of the kids and their families; then we'll see what you think." So he says, "Well, all right, I'll do it, but I can't do it for nothing." We said, "You've got to do it for nothin' or the idea won't work." He says, "Well, how about I give you the air time, but you cover my production costs. My bosses won't tolerate me spending their money and going into the red." We stopped pushing at that point; we were pretty sure we'd gotten the best deal we were going to get.

Next, we went to the largest children's hospital in L.A. Believe it or not, this was a harder sell than the television station. We found that to be true with most of the hospitals we visited in the early days. They felt they were above "going on public TV to beg for money." This particular hospital was extremely conservative. They were very concerned about their reputation and careful about where their money came from. We let them know that 100 percent of the money raised would go to their hospital. We also assured them that the show would be done with 100 percent dignity and class, with no kids being exploited. They finally agreed to jump in and see what would happen.

From there we went to a number of other markets: Vegas, Reno, Dallas, Oklahoma City, and others. Each week, Joe would do five cities and I would do five cities. We tried to schedule three appointments each day. On Saturdays and Sundays we would discuss people's reactions to our program and think up ways to make it more appealing. Then we'd hit the road again for another week. We really didn't have much time to plan—we just flew like crazy! And we did it all with donated airplane tickets, which didn't always offer the best connections. I remember one time flying from Boise to Twin Falls to Salt Lake to Denver to Memphis to Huntsville to finally reach Atlanta. We also lacked money and weren't getting paid. I was thirty-two years old and had spent my whole career working for the March of Dimes—you're not gonna get rich there. [Laughs.] We figured we could last for six months with the free tickets and hotels.

We just had faith that the phone bill would somehow get paid. We actually kept this pace up for three years, which was how long it took to cover the whole country.

During that first year, we started looking for sponsors to support us. It was difficult until we had a base of hospitals and stations in place. Of course, Western and Marriott were great! Then we met a guy named Brett Hutchens who was about our same age. [Chuckles.] He was president of Duff's Smorgasbord Restaurants. Homer and Wilma Duff owned the business and had hired Brett to run it. They had like 250 restaurants in the Midwest at the time. Brett is a real entrepreneur and immediately caught our vision. Joe asked him for $150,000 to pay some bills and keep us going. Right on the spot, Brett says, "I'm good for it." At the time, we only had stations in seven of the markets in which Duff's was doing business, so they weren't going to receive a real business benefit. But Brett brought a check for $150,000 to our first show. As we were walking off the stage, he pulled me aside and said, "I'm good for this next year, too." Since then, he has brought us Wal-Mart, Food Lion, some drugstores, and a number of other sponsors as well. They are all great people who are willing to make things happen.

That first year we finally got twenty-two hospitals and thirty television stations on board. We produced one main show that was broadcast by all the stations. We did it live out of the Osmonds' studio in Provo, Utah. The president of the studio, Bill Critchfield agreed to let us use it for free—there was no way we could have paid for it. Our stars that year were Marie Osmond and John Schneider (our celebrity co-founders), plus Marilyn McCoo and Merlin Olsen. The whole Osmond family was there as well. It was a great team. We broadcasted live for twenty-one hours—forty minutes of national and twenty minutes of local each hour. The phones were all manned at the local stations, and the checks were written directly to the hospitals in each area.

We generated nearly $5 million that first year. Then it really took off. We did $12 million the next year, then $29 million, and so on. We are now in every market in North America. We have 170 hospitals on board and 200 television stations, and we'll raise about $200 million this year. About half of this money comes from our telethon campaign; the other half comes from our corporate sponsors. These sponsors don't actually write out checks. What they do is appoint someone in their company to manage a campaign. We then link them with the hospitals, provide training materials, and supply anything else they need to get the job done. So it's really their people getting excited about kids in the community and raising money for their local hospital. Wal-Mart will bring in about $30 million this year. Re/Max, Dairy Queen, Amoco, and others are also great sponsors. It's a real win-win deal as long as everyone understands that the kids come first. We make this absolutely clear from the very beginning. If everyone agrees, we can help corporations create very successful programs to meet both their business and social objectives.

Our telethon has really evolved over the years. In 1987, we moved it from Provo, Utah, to Disneyland. Then in 1996, we moved it to Walt Disney World. We still have twenty-one hours of live programming over the weekend. In the evening, we have concerts to hold people's attention—Amy Grant, Kenny Loggins, and John Tesh. This year we're trying a new twist with the rock band Styx. On Sunday morning we show educational programs on a variety of topics like self-esteem, nutrition, fitness, how to install car seats, air-bag safety, and so on. We've now added other programs as well, so we're not totally reliant on the weekends. We have nine, thirty-minute magazine packages, twelve cable shows, and a radio-thon each year.

Over the years, we've held firm to our commitment to leave 100 percent of the funds in each local community. Hospitals use this money to buy all kinds of expensive and sophisticated equipment: ventilators, iso-labs, blood-transfusion machines, and so on. We've even paid the salaries of specialists the hospital could not afford otherwise. None of the dollars we raise are used to support our own organization. We receive our funds from several sources. First, each of our hospitals pays a small annual fee for the right to its market. This makes the hospitals the recipients of everything we do: the stations, the programming, the corporate campaigns, and of course, all the money we raise in their area. These fees make up less than half of our budget; the rest comes from a handful of corporations that generously underwrite our efforts.

The best part of this work is seeing our impact on the kids. I could sit here all day and tell you story after story about children we have helped. One that touched me pretty strongly was Daniel Dyer from Nashville, Tennessee. Daniel had leukemia and was not expected to live a year. He brought his little guitar with him and played a song on our show. He was six years old, bald from chemotherapy, and cute as a button. The next year he was back singing the same song with a full head of hair in complete remission. Today, he's going to college at Vanderbilt.

There's another kid from Dayton, Ohio, named Ahad Israfael. When he was fifteen years old he was working in a pizza shop, and some guy came in and robbed the place. The store manager got a gun and went after the guy. When the manager came back to put the gun away, it accidentally fired and literally blew half of Ahad's head off! It was a real tragedy, to say the least! The amount of damage that was done was just incredible! Ahad got the best attention possible in one of our hospitals, and today he's doing fine. He called me a while back and said, "Mick, guess what? I just graduated from high school!" A while later, "Mick, I'm going to college!" Each time he calls I tell him, "I knew you could do it." He has now graduated from college and is starting his own business. It just goes to show what faith and support from others can do for a person!

I think one of the reasons we've been successful is that we run this organization on good old-fashioned business principles. You can have all the passion in the world, but if you can't produce a return on people's investment of time and money, you won't last. If you don't last, you can't help anyone. One of the first things Joe and I did was create a board of directors and concede authority to them. This is not about two guys trying to make a living or create wealth for themselves. Our board of directors runs the organization, and we listen to them very carefully. They study our financial statements and hold us accountable. We always try to get the highest return possible on everything we do. We don't measure success by how many employees we have or the size of our budget. We'll continue to pursue our objectives as efficiently as possible.

> You can have all the passion in the world, but if you can't produce a return on people's investment of time and money, you won't last.

Another key to our success has been an unwavering focus on our mission. From day one, our number-one objective has been taking care of children. Every decision we make, every action we take, every strategy we adopt is based on what's best for the kids. No egos and no business objectives will ever get in the way of that. We work with some of the biggest names in America— Garth Brooks, Steve Young, John Elway, Michelle Kwan, Rebecca Lobo, many of the Miss Americas—and they all leave their egos home. None of these people ever gets paid, and we don't do limousines. They all make tremendous contributions because they buy into our mission. I think this really sums up what we're all about. We are enablers who harness people's hearts and talents toward a common goal: serving the children of North America. We've really built this organization with people power.

PETER GOLD

Peter Gold and his partner, Kyle Zimmer, are the founders of First Book, an organization with a simple mission: to provide books to disadvantaged children who have never had one—new books they can put their names in and never have to give back.

The organization works with existing community literacy programs to serve the hardest-to-reach children: those in shelters, community youth centers, and public housing programs. First Book's success results from a network of partnerships with businesses like Barnes & Noble Books, B. Dalton Bookseller, Scholastic, the Corporation for Public Broadcasting, and many others.

In 1984 an old friend and I opened the Washington, D.C., office of the Wall Street law firm of Winthrop, Stimson, Putnam & Roberts. I was a partner there for ten years. One of my clients during this time was the Navajo Nation. While working with the Navajo people, I gained a much greater awareness of the literacy problem in the United States. At the same time, I was on the board of directors of Share Our Strength, the hunger-relief organization started by Billy Shore. It was pretty clear to us that children have a very difficult time concentrating in school when their bellies are empty. I started feeling like we might be losing an entire generation.

One of my associates who worked with the Navajo Nation was Kyle Zimmer, who later became the cofounder of First Book and now serves as its president. One day in May of 1992, Kyle came into my office with Liz Arky, another associate working on Navajo issues. Kyle had just returned from a one-year sojourn in Seattle, Washington, where she had learned about an organization that provided new books to disadvantaged kids. Kyle and Liz suggested that we start a similar program in the District of Columbia. At the time, I was working on one of these mega-mergers that had many zeroes involved. [Laughs.] It struck me that as a partner in a Wall Street law firm, with the contacts my partners and I had, we could do something that was very needed and unique, not just in Washington, D.C., but nationally as well.

Kyle and Liz began doing research on literacy programs around the country and gathered a lot of information that helped us create our model. The first thing we decided to do was focus on disadvantaged kids: those in shelters for battered women and the homeless, family day-care agencies, public housing projects, programs associated with libraries, migrant worker centers, and so on. These kids seemed to be the hardest to reach and needed the most help. We wanted to give them their own first book, one they could put their name in and keep.

Second, we decided to work through existing community-based literacy programs. We had no intention of replicating the great work that was already being done in each local community. Instead, we wanted to reward effective programs by giving them the books they needed for their children. In particular, we wanted to support programs that had local heroes actively involved in tutoring and mentoring these kids. We felt that the bond between a mentor and the child was critical to the success of any program.

Third, we decided that the best way to achieve our objectives was to form partnerships with blue-chip companies that were the best in their areas; without their help, we knew it would take forever to grow to the size and effectiveness we desired. It was also important to us to have our corporate partners benefit beyond the realm of charitable rewards. In other words, we wanted this to be a sensible business proposition for them. One of the first companies we approached was Scholastic Books, one of the largest publishers of children's books in the world. We told them that the only way this new entity would work was if we could get deep discounts on their books, which they agreed to give. They also agreed to provide up to 5,000 free books to each new community we entered. This has allowed us to go to any city in the United States and say, "We have books for you, and we can start pretty quickly!"

Finally, we decided that decisions about which programs to support and what books to provide should be left to the local experts. If you combined the knowledge of Kyle and me about literacy and children's books, you'd probably only be able to fill a small children's book. [Laughs.] So what we've done is form local advisory groups in every community consisting of people with common and vested interests. These are typically parents, teachers, community leaders, bookstore managers, and so forth. We get these people together and ask them two questions: "Which are the best literacy programs in your community?" and "Who else should be sitting around this table with us?" These advisory boards provide all the guidance necessary to make the program work in their area.

Overall, our model has worked very well. We've grown significantly since our beginning. In 1992, our first year, we distributed about 12,000 books. In 1998, we were in more than 200 communities and gave out 2.4 million new books. By the end of this year, we expect to be in 300 communities and distribute more than 3 million books. We now have dozens of great partners, including Scholastic, Barnes & Noble, B. Dalton, Random House, Corporation for Public Broadcasting, Association for Library Service to the Children of the American Library Association, Hearst Magazines, Kiwanis, and many others. We have fifteen paid staff and sixteen volunteers from the AmeriCorps*Vista Program. Our administrative costs run as low as 3 to 4 percent of our annual budget.

Our corporate partners deserve a lot of credit—they have been a real key to our success! Billy Shore at Share Our Strength provided a $10,000 grant to help us get started. In addition, my law firm—Winthrop, Stimson, Putnam & Roberts—has donated hundreds of thousands of dollars of attorney time over the years. Barnes & Noble has also been a great partner; they have donated everything from cash to printing to establishing First Book Children's Hours in their stores. Once a month they bring in disadvantaged children, give them books, feed them, and read to them. Now, each time they open a new superstore, they donate 10 percent of the first day's proceeds to First Book. Interestingly, Barnes & Noble has never asked us for anything in return. We have to tell their story to the press because they don't seek credit themselves. We'll do that for any of our partners because they deserve it; that's what a true partnership is all about; it's a win/win situation.

Along with great partners, our program succeeds because the model works. A study done by Lou Harris & Associates shows that the children who receive these new books show a significant increase in school performance. One of the most dramatic stories was an experience Kyle and I had with children from a local shelter. We took them to a bookstore in an affluent section of Washington, D.C., and let them buy any combination of books they wanted worth ten dollars. Afterward, we took them to a really nice restaurant and let them order whatever they wanted, an experience most of them had never had before. Even though there were touching moments, we wondered if anything would ever come of the experience.

> A study done by Lou Harris & Associates shows that the children who receive these new books show a significant increase in school performance.

About three months later we got a call from the owner of the bookstore. She said, "If you ever wonder about the effectiveness of First Book, let me tell you this story." She told us that one of the kids from the shelter came back to the store with his tutor. The little boy asked the owner, "Do you remember me?" Well, the store owner did remember the boy. The tutor told the store owner that this boy was one of the brightest kids in her class, but the previous month his brother had been shot and killed right in front of him. He was becoming very morose and withdrawn, so the tutor told him she would take him anywhere he wanted: a Bullets game, the zoo, the park. Well, the boy said he wanted to go back to the Cheshire Cat Book Store. [Laughs.] After hearing this, the owner told the boy he could pick any four books he wanted. Then she asked him if he wanted to work at the cash register for a while. With help, the boy spent the next three hours ringing out customers. He left the store beaming!

Another time there were two unrelated kids from the same classroom. They were average students, but they always tried. One day they both went to the back of the room and stopped trying all together. The teacher found out that they were depressed because each of their parents had been arrested. She tried to re-engage them, but nothing worked. One day they were back at the front of the class and all the students were swarming around them. They had these new books from First Book, which they received from a children's literacy program at the prison. The books had labels in them that said, "This book belongs to . . ." with their names written on the label. Their friends were all fascinated with these books. For the last seven weeks of school, both these kids were at the front of the class, participating regularly. We hear stories like this all the time.

Anyway, when we started First Book, I thought the books themselves would be a ray of hope and optimism for kids who have very little. And while the books are important, I've realized that the relationship between the mentor and the child is the critical part of the program. The bond that develops lets the child know that someone cares, which produces the motivation for learning.

What our program does is get high-level corporate people to sit down with people from all parts of the city. The interaction that results dramatically changes people's perceptions about problems facing people from different cultures and economic classes. It is a beginning step toward solving our social problems. It starts with First Book, then spreads to other issues. There is so much untapped potential out there. We have found that people respond when they are asked. They don't always respond with money, but they respond with their skills, time, and compassion. I think this type of service should be required in America at some time in a person's life. Maybe we can call it the price of free citizenship.

The most vivid demonstration of how this program has affected me is the fact that I gave up my lucrative job at the law firm to spend more time doing it. There have definitely been risks, but it's been worth it to me. I wasn't really sure where we were going at first, but I knew that with common sense, hard work, and goodwill we could achieve most anything. Our organization shows what can happen when cooperative minds get together and recognition is irrelevant. Our goal continues to be to serve millions of disadvantaged kids around the country by giving them their first new books.

HARRY GRANADER

Harry Granader and his wife, Sylvia, are the founders of Camp Mak-A-Dream, a camp for children with cancer and other serious blood diseases. The camp occupies eighty-seven acres of a working cattle ranch in Montana. The camp is free of charge to the families of the children who participate. Since opening in 1995, Camp Mak-A-Dream has given hundreds of children with serious illnesses the opportunity to make friends, build good memories, and enjoy life as other children do. Here's Harry's story:

In 1960, I got a McDonald's Hamburger Franchise in the lower part of Detroit. McDonald's started in 1955, so we were one of the early franchises. I think they had about 100 locations at the time. About ten years ago, I retired and gave my eight stores to my son Gary.

While I had my stores, McDonald's started opening Ronald McDonald Houses all over the United States. These houses are for parents to stay in while their children are being treated at the hospital. I volunteered to help them get one started in Detroit next to Children's Hospital. Before we could build the house, we had to raise funds. What we did was sell milkshakes and donate all the money to this cause. We raised $300,000 within a month! So we got the architects and builders together and built the house.

After we did the house in Detroit, I got a call from a hospital in Ann Arbor. They said, "We would like to have a Ronald McDonald House." I asked if they had the finances to take care of it, and they said no. So I said, "I'll go to the bank and borrow $500,000, and I hope you can pay it back within a year." They agreed to do so and built their house. They were able to pay me back through community fund-raising.

While these houses were being built, I would visit the hospitals and see these children . . . [Becomes emotional.] You'll have to excuse me, I get pretty sentimental. I saw children with heart disease, kidney disorders, leukemia, cancer, and other serious diseases. I also saw kids who were four or five years old on dialysis machines. I was really touched and knew I had to do something for these children. That's how I got the idea of building a camp.

I own a ranch in Montana because I like the outdoors. So I dedicated eighty-seven acres of property plus $300,000 to start the camp. I also sold another ranch I had and loaned the money to the foundation. In addition, we found people in Missoula, Montana—which is about sixty miles away—who wanted to help with fund-raising and construction. They contacted people all over Montana and held fund-raising events. Since the whole state of Montana only has 600,000 people, we also went to other states, knowing that children from all over the country would attend the camp. My son Gary contacted a company in Chicago, and they held an auction that raised about $100,000. Then the McDonald's Corporation gave us some money. We found a company that wanted to do the construction at cost, so we started building. This was in 1993.

The camp opened in the summer of 1995. Volunteers put in hundreds of hours painting, cleaning, and getting the grounds ready. The governor came and congratulated the 1,000 heroes who made the camp possible—money-raisers, donors, planners, builders. The camp consists of an 11,000-square-foot main lodge and four beautiful cabins. Each cabin has a fireplace in the center and beds for sixteen children on the sides. They also have a kitchen and a room for two counselors. So we can have about sixty kids here any given week. Our plans call for six cabins, but we haven't raised enough money yet.

That first summer, forty-six children came to camp; last year we had more than 250. These are very special kids. They have a disease they do not want and treatment that is very painful. Most of them are hurting and need compassion and understanding. Regular summer camps won't take them if they are on chemotherapy or in a wheelchair, so their recreational activities are limited. Our goal is to give them some good times to help them through the bad times. We give them a chance to do what other kids do and free them from the isolation they experience. When they come to camp, they meet other children who have the same disease, and they make a lot of new friends. They aren't worried about being bald or about having one leg or one arm. It's a chance to get away from the emotions and challenges of their disease and be like regular kids. They really do forget they are sick for a week. I spent all last summer there . . . [Becomes emotional.] These children inspire me so much. We just can't do enough for them.

> When they come to camp, they meet other children who have the same disease, and they make a lot of new friends. They aren't worried about being bald or about having one leg or one arm.

The camp is open all summer, and we have different groups of children come. We have a Kid's Camp for children six to sixteen, and a Young Adult Conference for those seventeen to twenty-three. We also have a Sibling's Camp for the brothers and sisters of those who have cancer. They are sometimes neglected because the sick child gets all the attention in the home. While these kids are here they do a lot of different things. They can go horseback riding, hiking, boating, canoeing, swimming, and fishing. We have a ropes course and an archery range, and they can do arts and crafts and drama. It's surprising how talented some of these children are. Doing all these things is really therapeutic for them. It's unbelievable. I can't explain it. You have to be at the camp to see what's going on. They keep saying, "This is a dream come true!" Most of them want to come back again. I get letters from them that all touch me. It really hurts when some of them pass away; about forty of them have died since being at the camp. The directors really surprised me last summer. They created a place called "Granader Gardens" that is dedicated to these children.

All of our counselors, doctors, and nurses are volunteers. They come from all over the United States, including Alaska, and they stay for a week or two at their own expense. They are wonderful, enthusiastic people. They all have things they want to fulfill in their own lives, and serving these children makes them feel so much better—so it works both ways. This is one of the reasons the camp is so successful. We also have a small staff that stays all summer. One of them is a doctor and co-director of the camp. We have a fully equipped medical infirmary that is staffed twenty-four hours a day by the doctors and nurses. If any of the children have problems, we have a heliport and can get them to a nearby hospital quickly. In addition, we have about forty people now serving on our board of directors.

The camp is free to the families of the children who come here, so we still have to raise money for operations. Knowing we couldn't do it all in Montana, we started a chapter in Michigan called Friends of Camp Mak-A-Dream. Our first year we raised about $70,000, and this year we will raise close to $150,000. Last summer we had a counselor at camp who liked it so much she went back home and set up a chapter in Spokane, Washington. So people learn about us and get interested. All of our donations come from individuals, corporations, and foundations. We have never received any money from the government.

A lot of people still don't know we are even in existence. So our other co-director, who is a registered nurse, goes to conferences all over the country and tells people about the camp. This is how we get most of the children. When hospitals find out about us, they start referring their kids. Last summer we had about twenty-five states represented at the camp—nearly forty kids came from Michigan alone. We think our numbers will continue to grow because we are open all summer, and even some weeks in the winter. A lot of camps are only open for one week. When the children aren't at the camp, we have other events. A couple of years ago we had a conference that focused on kids with cancer who are seventeen to twenty-three years old. It was held for two days in February. We had people come from Texas, Connecticut, California, Utah, Washington, and Kansas. They were all cancer specialists, doctors, nurses, and directors from other camps. The purpose was to share information, find out what these kids need, and build relationships between programs. This year we had a Caregivers' Conference for professional health-care providers, and several conferences for men and women with different types of cancer.

It's taken a lot of people to accomplish what we have. I never could have done it alone. My wife has been with me all along and feels the same way I do. We can't do enough for these kids. Helping them has been one of the most rewarding experiences of our lives. I'm eighty-two years of age right now—I don't ever say "old." I feel that God is looking after me . . . [becomes emotional] and he wants me to do a lot of good deeds before I leave. I keep telling everybody, "I'm so far behind, I'm going to be here for a long time." I'm pretty sentimental. But I believe the more you share the more you will have. So open a door for somebody else. In one of my speeches I quoted Helen Keller. She said something like, "The most beautiful things in the world cannot be seen or even touched. They must be felt with the heart." By sharing a piece of your heart, you can improve the lives of many children.

CHAPTER · 3

TEACHING
OUR YOUTH

*Ignorance is the night of the mind, but a night without moon or
star.*

CONFUCIUS

*Train up a child in the way he should go: and when he is old, he
will not depart from it.*

PROVERBS 22:6

*The greatest discovery of my generation is that human beings can
alter their lives by altering their attitudes of mind.*

WILLIAM JAMES

Broad-shouldered, over six feet tall and 200-plus pounds, Rey Lucas was
a big kid, especially for a ninth grader. And he carried a big load on his
shoulders. Both his parents struggled with serious illnesses, and neither
was able to work. Rey was chiefly responsible for the care of his baby
sister. During this bleak period, the family barely got by on disability payments.

To complicate matters, Rey thought he wasn't very smart, and
because he was dyslexic, he worried about how he would make a living himself some day. His size was his only hope—if he could just
become a pro football player, perhaps he'd find a way out. Besides,

football allowed him to unleash all his worries and anger, and no one minded.

Biology was another matter. His teacher, Tammy Bird, minded a lot when Rey got into fights or threw things. One day he was so out of control she had to call for an off-duty police officer to calm him down. Fortunately, Ms. Bird minded in other ways, too. It bothered her that Rey had no idea how smart he was, or how persistent. Rey kept coaxing people to let him enter the school's garden program, Food From the 'Hood, a project the students had started to provide fresh vegetables for their inner-city neighbors. Normally, ninth graders weren't accepted into the program, but Rey wouldn't take no for an answer. He worked hard, and his classmates grew to admire other things besides his physical strength—like his honesty and common sense. Whenever his anger and worries threatened to overwhelm him, his new friends would say, "Rey, go take a walk in the garden."

In tenth grade, Rey was injured in football and started spending even more time in the garden and biology room. He studied so much that of 200 students, he scored the highest on a biology lab practicum. Ms. Bird was elated. "I photocopied his test and stapled it all over the Food From the 'Hood office," she said. Encouraged by his success, Rey soon learned to use the office computer to create banners, flyers, and logos for Food From the 'Hood. He got so good at graphic arts, he even made the organization's Christmas cards.

"By the time Rey hit eleventh grade, the kids began seeing him as the heart of the program because he worked so hard and would give you the shirt off his back," says Ms. Bird. "Like his name, he really was our ray of sunshine. Wherever Rey went, people listened to him. He radiated such presence. His big smile just lit up the room."

Rey discovered he had other talents as well. On a student trip to the Social Ventures Network Conference in New York, Ms. Bird loaned Rey her camera and asked him to serve as the students' photographer. Businesses like Ben & Jerry's and Patagonia liked his photos so much, they asked him to serve as the official conference photographer the following year. Unfortunately, Rey had to decline—he was too busy at Orange Coast College.

Today Rey is working to become a teacher and coach, as well as a photographer. His investment points from working at Food From the 'Hood paid for his first camera and some of his college expenses. The big ninth grader with big problems is now a young man with a bright future.

Early childhood experiences have a powerful impact on the emotional and chemical makeup of our youth. Debra Niehoff, author of *The Biology of Violence*, explains, "Although people are born with some biological givens, the brain has many blank pages. From the first moments of childhood the brains acts as a historian, recording our experiences in the language of neurochemistry." If young children receive unconditional love and support from their parents—and hopefully from extended family members and schoolmates—they develop an adequate self-esteem and the ability to form healthy relationships. On the other hand, children raised in neglectful and abusive environments can become crippled emotionally and physiologically.

According to Dr. Bruce Perry of Baylor College of Medicine, children who suffer a repeated barrage of emotional stress actually experience changes in their brain chemistry. The constant flood of stress chemicals tends to reset the brain's fight-or-flight hormones at higher levels, resulting in hair-trigger emotions and impulsive-aggressive tendencies. When real or perceived threats occur—name calling, a shove, an elbow in the stomach—these kids can respond with abnormally violent behavior.

Perry also found that early neglect and mistreatment can inhibit the development of the brain's cortex, which governs the emotions of attachment and belonging. As a protective strategy to alleviate the constant pain, the emotions of these kids simply shut down, resulting in antisocial tendencies. Lacking empathy and sensitivity to the world around them, antisocial youth can abuse other people with no regret whatsoever.

Whether the response to an emotionally toxic environment is aggression or antisocial behavior, the result is the same: these youth feel alienated and ostracized. The only difference between them is that impulsive aggressors feel sorry after their aggression, while antisocial aggressors feel nothing at all. Experts believe we have legions of these unattached kids walking around our schools and cities.

Along with alienation, our youth are exposed to a constant diet of violence in the media. Murder, brutal behavior, and dark-side pursuits are the common themes of television shows, movies, and video games. Many kids who lack the counterbalancing voice of loving parents or guardians grow up believing that violence is the way to solve their problems and get revenge. Ironically, when violent tragedies occur, the media "over-reports" the mayhem as a form of entertainment, which reinforces the culture that created the violent acts in the first place. It's a tragic cycle that fuels our violence-ridden society. Unfortunately, when disconnected kids with easy access to weapons experience an overdose of violence, the results can be disastrous.

Statistics that reflect our current state of affairs are staggering. Nearly 10 percent of all high-school students have taken a weapon to school; 135,000 have taken a gun into their classrooms; 31 percent have seen another student carrying a gun; 15 percent report being victimized at school; and 63 percent of all Americans now feel that a shooting incident could occur at their local schools. In addition, 25 percent of all males arrested for violent crimes in America—for murder, rape, or assault—are under the age of eighteen; 25 percent of adolescents arrested for violent crimes are girls; and juvenile homicide is now twice as common as it was ten years ago. Equally alarming, more than 2,400 kids are calling it quits and dropping out of school every day in America, and suicide is the second leading cause of death for fifteen- to nineteen-year-olds.

To temper the pain of detachment, many of our youth are join-ing gangs. Gangs now exist in all fifty states, and not just in large cities like Los Angeles, New York, and Chicago but also in midsized cities like Albuquerque, Fort Wayne, and Louisville. In Los Angeles alone, gang membership has more than doubled in the past decade—from 450 gangs with 40,000 members to nearly 1,000 gangs with more than 120,000 members. Gangs tend to spring up in disenfranchised neighborhoods that suffer from overcrowding, poverty, and high unemployment. Kids join gangs to obtain recog-nition, feelings of belonging, discipline, and money. Gang members are typically thirteen- to twenty-four-year-old males, although female membership is increasing. Some experts estimate that more than 80 percent of these kids are functionally illiterate, with no hope of finding a job. Unfortunately, guns now decide arguments rather than fists, and gang wars resemble guerrilla warfare, with drive-by shootings and sniping from rooftops.

What these youth need are strong role models who show unconditional love, then stay around long enough for lasting change to occur. As William James observed, "Human beings can alter their lives by altering their attitudes of mind." Long-term success often requires a total reprogramming of values, attitudes, and feelings about self. Such a transformation takes time, but with a heavy dose of compassion and lots of support, troubled teens can become enthusiastic participants in America's grand experiment in freedom.

Here are the stories of five incredible people who are grappling with the problems faced by our youth. Tammy Bird helped her stu-dents at Crenshaw High School create Food From the 'Hood fol-lowing the race riots in Los Angeles; the program has helped numerous students like Rey Lucas learn business skills and earn money for college. Bill Strickland started the Manchester Craftsmen's Guild to motivate inner-city kids to stay in school; he uses the arts to increase their confidence and self-esteem. With the help of Michael Jordan, Stedman Graham launched Athletes Against

Drugs to teach leadership skills and keep kids off illicit substances. Meredith Blake created Break the Cycle to stem the tide of domestic and dating violence in our country. And Bill Halamandaris started The Heart of America to give kids new role models, teach them about community service, and help them obtain funds for college. Together these social entrepreneurs have saved thousands of young people from lives of hopelessness, failure, and destruction. More of us need to follow their example.

TAMMY BIRD

Science teacher Tammy Bird and ad executive Melinda McMullen helped Crenshaw High School students found Food From the 'Hood after the Los Angeles riots of 1992. Started as a campus garden, this student-owned business—which sells organic produce and two lines of salad dressing—provides food for the community's needy and funds for student scholarships— $130,000 since its inception. Business Week named Tammy's students "Entrepreneurs of the Year" in 1994, and Newsweek honored them with their American Achievement Award in 1995. Britain's Prince Charles has also toured their garden.

On my way to veterinary school, I stopped to teach science at Crenshaw High School, fell in love with the students, and never left. Besides teaching, I was the volleyball coach. But three years into the experience, I was tired of the four walls—I needed more space. While looking around campus, I found the old, abandoned Agricultural Center with remnants of a greenhouse, animal lab, and garden plots. It was totally trashed, but I fell in love with it—like my Secret Garden. The principal told me I could have it, so I spent the summer gutting it. When school started, I had my students help me fix it up and maintain it. We called it the Environmental Education Center and started a program called "Zoo on Wheels" where we taught children at local elementary schools about animals.

In the meantime, I tried to plant vegetables in the garden, but I'm a marine biologist. I didn't even know which way to plant stuff, so I started picking people's brains. I found a couple of little old lady volunteers whom we called our "Gardening Angels." So gardening became part of class. This was hands-on botany, zoology, and ecology every Friday. The kids learned to wear old clothes because "Ms. Bird made you go out in the garden and work." At the time, environmental education wasn't the "sexy" topic, but the State Education Agriculture Department was really interested in revitalizing urban agriculture. So I wrote up my idea for the Center using their agriculture buzzwords, and in 1988 got the first funding for tools and supplies for the garden.

I saw a real spark when the kids grew the vegetables. We entered some contests and won first place in *L.A. Beautiful* for a garden we represented in a drought situation. This went on for a while, but eventually all funding for agriculture programs in the city died. In 1990–91, our monetary support was gone, and our volunteer staff was drying up too. Even my contacts couldn't help.

One April day in 1992, I was riding back to the school on the bus with my men's volleyball team. When we hit the corner of Florence and Normandy, we saw all this ruckus—angry people running everywhere. I said to the bus driver, "Let's just run the red light and get out of here," because I had kids with me. When I got back to school, my boyfriend at the time, a police officer, phoned and said, "Turn on the TV!" So I turned on channel 11 and dropped the phone. I realized it was a riot and we had driven right through the middle of it. There was Crenshaw Boulevard in flames. If you ever watch TV clips of the riots, you can see our bus go through the intersection at Florence and Normandy—that's my men's volleyball team!

When the president came to visit the riot area, his first stop was four blocks from Crenshaw High. Things were so bad that school was closed for a week. I had to have a police escort take me to the

Animal Lab to care for our twenty rabbits, chickens, geese, ducks, and reptiles. When we got back to school the following week, a lot had changed. When I was first hired, I had to break barriers because I was young, white, female, and in science. But I succeeded and everything was cool. I thought I knew the people and the neighborhood. After the riots, I was a white person walking in a black neighborhood again. The color line had been drawn.

This period was a big turning point. My students and I tried to see where each other was coming from. After our "debriefing," and after the initial hurt was gone, we all sat down and said, "What are we gonna do?" During this time, people who had helped with the garden before started calling and saying, "Hey, look, I've got volunteers for you." "I've got these tools." "I've got these trees." So I said to the kids, "What do you think? We've got the help we need; let's get this garden back!" The students got really enthused; they showed up on a couple of Saturdays and started working.

In those days, we experienced what I call "The White Flight into the Inner City." A lot of white people came rushing in to take care of their guilt and then left. But some of them with hearts of gold truly wanted to make a difference and stayed to work. Melinda McMullen was one of them. Melinda was a PR executive from the community who was doing volunteer work for a group called Garden for Kids. When she visited our school, she said to me, "You know, the riots were about economics, not color. Why don't you turn your garden into a business?" I said, "Sure, but I need help. The students' interest in gardening only lasts about six months." And she said, "Well, let's present the idea to them. Maybe they'll want to turn it into a business." I thought, "That'd be cool. If it's their idea, they'll have the ownership."

So we presented the idea to the kids, and they were really excited. The ones who decided to participate were an eclectic group. The population at Crenshaw High at the time was 80 percent African-American, 17 percent Latin, and 3 percent "other," so you just didn't see a mixture. But our group was a real tossed salad. We had black kids, brown kids, and Asian kids coming together. We had "A" students, jocks and cheerleaders, brown-nosers who wanted extra credit, and kids who were just trying to keep their heads above water. We had tenth graders working with twelfth graders, and the computer nerd working alongside the football jock. The kids felt really good about it because they were creating this beautiful, green spot.

One of the first things we did was name the garden. We brought in pizza and had a brainstorming session. The kids listed more than seventy names on the chalkboard, then narrowed the list down to twelve. They did market research by asking friends, relatives, and people all over town what they thought. *Food From the 'Hood* was their first choice. Next, they needed a logo, so two artists in the group got input from their classmates, then came back with a drawing of two hands—one brown and one white—with a sprout in the middle and the sun in the background. It was very simple and very symbolic. It also had a great mix of colors: blue, gold, brown, white, and green.

We still weren't sure what direction we'd take, but the energy and enthusiasm were incredible. Here was this group of students and two adults trying to figure things out. I had the kid sense and knew the school district. Melinda understood public relations and helped with the business stuff. As a teacher, I always look at the world through rose-colored glasses, and Melinda gave me that reality check, which was cool. We made a good team that way. For a long time we were really covert because there are so many rules and regulations when you're part of a large school district. But I kept thinking, "This is positive; the students are learning; it's a healing process." It just felt too good to stop.

We wanted to grow organic vegetables because we thought it would help the community. Before the riots, the grocery stores in South Central L.A. were really poor. They just had wilted lettuce and a few varieties of produce. To show the kids the possibilities, we visited Mrs. Gooch's grocery store. This really cool African-American guy who was a vegetarian told us about all the different types of food and loaded up two baskets for us. When we left, the kids said, "We're hungry. Can we go to McDonald's or Burger King?" Melinda and I said, "You guys, we've got all this healthy food here. Let's have a picnic in the park." And they responded, "We want some real food." Melinda and I just looked at each other and said, "Oh, we've got a lot of work to do."

We started off with three objectives. The first was to create a green spot in the garden. The second was to donate healthy food to the needy in the community. The third was to sell vegetables and use the profits to provide scholarships for the kids. In December of 1992 we had our first harvest, and on Christmas Eve we packed dozens of boxes of vegetables for a local food bank. We were on our way to realizing our objectives.

Meanwhile, Melinda and I were learning a lot of things on the fly. We found out we had to incorporate and got a law firm to help us. We also started writing grants to raise some money. Melinda is a great grant writer, and we received funding from the Community Development Department for books, field trips, and things like that. Up to that point, we had been funding Food From the 'Hood out of our own pockets. About this time, we decided we'd try selling produce at the farmers' market, so we had to get certified by the State Agriculture Department. They told us we could sell vegetables but not fruit because we were in a fruit-fly quarantine area. So much for our tomato crop—but the chickens, duck, geese, and iguanas had a feast!

On a spring morning in 1993, we took our first produce to the farmers' market in Santa Monica. Most of the sellers there are older and either Latin or White. All of a sudden these "Hip Hop" kids from the inner city are trying to sell their vegetables. Most of the customers wouldn't even come near them. Not to be discouraged, one of our students stood out in the middle of the walkway and said, "Hi, I'm Ben. We're students at Crenshaw High School earning money for college. Welcome to Food From the 'Hood!" He started shaking people's hands and bringing them over to the stand. Next thing you know, the kids are telling people all about their program and selling vegetables—it was really inspiring. Their self-esteem was shooting so high you could see their shoulders stand up.

At the end of the day, they're counting their money and saying, "We've got $300 sittin' here!" I looked at them holding the $300 and said, "Okay, I need this much for gas and this much for the awning we just bought." Then Melinda said, "I need gas money too, plus what we paid for the vegetables. And let's see, how many of you guys worked in the garden for three months to make this happen? Well, you just made about twenty cents an hour." We watched their faces drop, but we wanted them to see reality.

In the months that followed, we got better at the farmers' market. Sometimes we didn't have very much to sell, so we had to be creative. One time we had a ton of collard greens, which aren't real popular in Santa Monica. So the kids came up with a recipe card explaining how to cook them, and they were a hit! We kept doing the farmers' market because it was fun and we were making money. All that Food From the 'Hood was at the time was the name, the garden, and the classroom. Melinda had gone part-time with her job and was giving lots of hours to the business. I was still teaching full-time, and the kids were working around their schedules. We were all juggling. [Laughs.]

After a while we started getting tons of press because everyone was looking for positive stories coming out of the riots. People would read about us, then call up and ask, "What can I do to help?" Just when we'd hit a brick wall, the phone would ring and someone would walk through the door—it was like God sent these people. It was absolutely amazing! And most of them had ideas for us. Some suggested we should create a product the way Paul Newman did. So the seed was planted. The kids did some research and found out that salad dressing was one of the fastest-growing products in the food industry. They finally decided to produce an Italian dressing because it was the most popular flavor at the time.

So I had a lab in my classroom. We brought in vinegars, oils, and all types of bottles. We picked herbs and vegetables from the garden and made copies of the logo. And then for three-and-a-half hours, fortified by pizza, the students created prototypes. The kids on the football team came up with this beautiful jar of sun-dried tomatoes in oil and basil. Someone else created a rosemary-flavored vinegar. They just came up with a really neat array of products. After doing these prototypes, they decided to make a creamy Italian dressing that wouldn't separate and have to be shaken. They wanted to call it "Straight Out 'the Garden."

> Just when we'd hit a brick wall, the phone would ring and someone would walk through the door—it was like God sent these people.

We were fortunate at that time to have a relationship with Rebuild L.A., an organization that helped small businesses after the riots. They helped us find a manufacturer ten minutes away. The students worked with the food chemists six times to get the color, consistency, and chunk-size just right. Then they noticed that the sodium level was high and said, "Oh no, we need to lower the sodium because hypertension is a huge problem in African-American communities." I was just floored! I was teaching physiology and didn't know I was getting through to these guys! Here they were using the science they had learned. I was in hog heaven!

Now all we needed was the funding for production. We were still making money from our vegetables, but we weren't rich. We didn't have an office and were using the school phone to conduct business. Then in December of '93, a donor shows up—thanks to Rebuild L.A.—and hands the kids a $50,000 grant! They were so excited they couldn't see straight. A few days later, the phone rang and a guy says, "Hi, my name is Norris. I'd like to help the students sell their salad dressing." It was Norris Bernstein of Bernstein's Salad Dressing, who was now a marketing consultant. He gave us suggestions to make our product more salable and helped us contact brokers and distributors. Christmas that year was indeed a happy time.

Come January, we were just getting things off the ground when the big Northridge Earthquake hit (no pun intended). Actually, the earthquake turned out to be positive for Food From the 'Hood because we got a week off from school. We moved all the rabbits outside, gutted the animal lab, and painted the walls during the aftershocks. [Laughs.] The principal kept running down to make sure everyone was okay. A few days later, the kids picked out office furniture, some computers, and a fax machine; ordered an 800 number; and—voilà!—corporate offices! It still has a pretty earthy feel. The door opens right out to the chickens, so every time you call someone, you hear a rooster crow. The iguana and pig walk through the office regularly, and flies still hang out there for institutional memory. [Laughs.]

With a new office and funding in place, we produced our first run of salad dressing. Our food brokers were wonderful. They let the kids go on sales calls with them and make presentations to executives at the supermarkets. So they learned every aspect of the business from growing to selling. And the product was a huge hit. By April of '94, the two-year anniversary of the riots, our salad dressing was in 100 percent of the big supermarket chains in Southern California. A year later, our students received the American Achievement Award and made the cover of *Newsweek*. We all went to Washington, D.C., for a big awards show. It was a huge boost to the program.

From that point on, we really started to grow. We are now in twenty-six states and bring in $200,000 a year. We're still selling Straight Out 'the Garden Creamy Italian Salad Dressing, but we have a new improved version. We lowered the fat content from 19 percent to 9 percent based on feedback from our customers. So the kids are listening. We also added another flavor, a no-fat honey mustard, which is a big seller for us. I am still teaching full-time and helping out on the side. We now have a full-time executive director of Food From the 'Hood. We also have a couple of vans that were donated to us, one from Nissan and one from the British government. So it's a real business.

The way we manage the program has evolved over the years. At first, anyone who wanted to could volunteer to work. We soon realized that some of the kids were not pulling their weight, so the students came up with a process for selecting members. They developed an application that included an essay and a copy of the person's report card. There is also an oral interview and an internship program for anyone selected. Ninth, tenth, and eleventh graders have to put in a minimum of seven hours a week. The seniors, who have a lot of extracurricular activities, are required to work at least five hours a week. So a student can enter the program in ninth grade and work all four years.

In the beginning we had a president, CEO, and COO of the company. We soon found out that the power went to the kids' heads, so we decided to become a consensus-type company. What we do is have a business meeting once a week, and all the kids in the program show up. To make a decision, we need a quorum of x number of votes. The people who end up with the power are the ones who do the most work. The seniors generally end up being the leaders and spokespeople because they have the most experience. The process works pretty well. If there's ever a conflict or discipline problem, I step in and put my foot down. But for the most part, the kids handle everything.

Since one of our objectives was to generate college funds for the kids, we had to develop a system for distributing the money. What we did was create a point system. You get points for each hour you work, points if you take the lead in a project, and extra points if you work beyond your weekly minimum. At the end of the fiscal year, we add up all the points and give each student a percentage of the whole universe. This is their percentage of the profits we earned that year. To actually get the money, they have to go on to higher education. It can be a trade school, a realty school, a cosmetology school, a two-year college, or a four-year university. We never hand the money directly to the students. They bring us invoices, and we write checks for their tuition, housing, computers, books, and so forth. To date we've had sixty-six students graduate from the program, and we've given out about $130,000 worth of scholarship money. It's not enough to support anyone through a four-year degree, but it gets kids started who may not attend college otherwise.

This has really been an amazing experience, although it's taken a lot of perseverance. You can't have thin skin and survive. Let me tell you a fun story. We heard that Prince Charles was coming to L.A. and knew that he liked youth projects. So we dropped off a letter at the British Consulate inviting him to our garden. A few weeks later, they called and said the Prince of Wales would be delighted to visit. Just three weeks before he came, the students opened the office and found it in shambles. Windows were broken and cables were torn from the wall. The thieves had taken our computers, fax machines, printers, everything. Most of the kids felt their dreams were over. But Ben was unfazed. He stood up and said, "What doesn't kill you makes you stronger. We'll come back better than ever." And come back they did. Within twenty-four hours, Food From the 'Hood was back in business, thanks to community contributions of over $15,000. It's remarkable to see how far we've come. Our motto: Plant a seed and watch what happens!

BILL STRICKLAND

Bill Strickland is one of America's most creative social entrepreneurs. He is the founder of the Manchester Craftsmen's Guild, an organization that uses the arts to motivate inner-city youth in Pittsburgh to stay in school and go to college. Approximately 80 percent of Bill's students enter undergraduate university programs. Bill is also the president of the Bidwell Training Center, a vocational school that helps economically disadvantaged individuals enter the workforce. Bidwell enjoys a 75 percent placement rate. In addition, Bill operates a Grammy-winning recording venture, a food service company and a real-estate division—each of which produces revenue for his social causes. Bill has received a Genius Grant from the MacArthur Foundation and a Coming Up Taller Award from the White House. Here's his story:

I grew up in the inner city of Pittsburgh and went to Oliver High School. When I was a tenth grader, I was walking down the hall and saw a teacher making ceramics in the art room. I went over to him and said, "I've never seen anything like that in my life. I want to learn to do it." He said, "Get your home-room teacher to sign a permission slip and I'll be glad to teach you." I got the signature and started making ceramics with Mr. Ross. I soon discovered I was very good with clay, so I cut my classes during the next two years to work in the art room. I gave all my pots to the teachers whose classes I cut, and they gave me passing grades. That's how I graduated.

That experience totally changed my life. Before I met Mr. Ross, I was way off track. I was probably on my way to jail, getting my head shot off, or being unemployed. I was basically a good kid, but I was unfocused. When you're a minority kid in the inner city you can't be unfocused, because it places you in jeopardy. Making ceramics with Mr. Ross was a real shot of adrenaline. It got me excited about learning and showed me I had value. It gave me a whole new vision of how life could be, and I set out to build that picture.

During my senior year, Mr. Ross took me out to the University of Pittsburgh and helped me fill out an application, in pencil. I got into Pitt on probation and eventually got a degree in history. It was during my freshman year in 1968 that I started the Manchester Craftsmen's Guild. My goal was to reproduce my life-transforming experience with Mr. Ross with other inner-city kids. I wanted to have what happened to me happen to them. I thought the arts could give these underprivileged kids the sense of importance they badly needed. I wasn't as interested in turning them into master craftsmen as I was in increasing their confidence and motivation. I used the term *guild* to reflect the Middle-Age concept of masters and apprentices working together in nurturing relationships.

I started off in a row house donated by the Episcopal Diocese. The bishop liked me a whole lot and let me use this old house, which I renovated with my father's help. I ran the program on the first floor and in the basement, and I lived upstairs. From day one, it was real easy to find the kids—they were all through the neighborhood. I just hung out a shingle and started dragging them in off the streets in order to save their lives. I had clay, I had wheels, and I had a kiln. Two Episcopal churches gave me the initial operating money to get started.

During the first few years things grew pretty well. I took another row house, fixed it up, and started a photography program based on the same concept. Anyone who wanted to learn ceramics or photography was welcome—and there was no shortage of kids. Before long, I hired a couple of instructors. Then I started getting grants from the State Council of the Arts and eventually the National Endowment for the Arts. Several local corporations and foundations also took notice and provided support. So things were off to a pretty good start.

In 1972 I took over the Bidwell Training Center. It was a big war-on-poverty program that was a total disaster—just like most poverty programs at the time. It was created to teach trade skills to people who were hard to employ. A lot of the students were laid-off workers from the steel industry. The center had courses in bricklaying, carpentry, wiring, mechanics—that kind of stuff. They were looking around for some fool to take it over, and I said, "Sure, I am Moses. I can save all the poor folks, no problem." It seemed like a good match with the Manchester Craftsmen's Guild, except it was a huge mess. My first day on the job, people were sitting on top of the desks, and half the toilets and fountains didn't work because all the copper had been taken out of the building. They also owed the Internal Revenue Service $300,000.

Over the next few years I rebuilt Bidwell from scratch. What I did was form partnerships with corporations that could benefit from our training: Bayer, IBM, Calgon Carbon, BASF, Blue Cross and Blue Shield, Nova Chemical, you name it. They provided curriculum development, technical personnel, and help with day-to-day operations. We also got accreditation from the State Department of Education, so we are a full-fledged vocational school. That means we get funding from the state and federal departments of education. Bidwell is now a multimillion-dollar, technology-oriented training center for poor people. We have programs in business travel, information sciences, medical technology, chemical technology, and the culinary arts. Anyone who wants to attend can do so for free, as long as they qualify under the economic guidelines of the state. They also have to have a good attitude, which is something you can't teach. Most of the students here recognize that this is their last stop—they are poor and lack self-confidence. We give them the encouragement they need to succeed. Our placement rate is over 75 percent pretty consistently.

At the same time I was building Bidwell, I was expanding the Manchester Craftsmen's Guild. We consolidated management, day-to-day operations, and funding wherever we could. In 1987 we moved both organizations into a new 62,000-square-foot facility. While Bidwell sends disadvantaged workers into the workforce,

Manchester sends kids to college. All eleven high schools in the Pittsburgh Public School System send me kids. Most are in after-school programs, but we have an integrated curriculum with one school, so their kids come at 9:00 A.M. and get credit for being here. We have courses in clay, photography, computer imaging, and jazz. Kids stay in these programs up to three years. We now have about 400 students, and we graduate fifty to sixty each year. These are all kids the system labels "at risk," but we operate on the assumption that nothing is wrong with them. I think that makes a big difference in how they see themselves. About 80 percent of these kids get into undergraduate programs all over the country. Nothing I'm aware of compares with our success rate.

These are all kids the system labels "at risk," but we operate on the assumption that nothing is wrong with them. I think that makes a big difference in how they see themselves.

Support for Manchester comes from several sources. We get public art funding from the National Endowment for the Arts and the Pennsylvania Council for the Arts. We also receive grants from private foundations like Heinz, Mellon, Hillman, and others. Then we have a host of great corporate sponsors like Bayer, Westinghouse, Alcoa, and PPG.

Our most important sources of money are probably those we're developing ourselves. I'm bright enough to know that you can't live off other people's funds forever, so we're doing some pretty neat things. We have a music hall where we do jazz concerts, big time! Dizzy Gillespie was the first guy to play here, then Billy Taylor, Count Basie, Wynton Marsalis, Nancy Wilson, Shirley Horn, Betty Carter—all the big names. Our concerts produce about $400,000 a year. I also hooked up a recording studio in the music hall, and with the permission of the artists, I record them. Bayer developed the plastic that compact discs are made of, so they've been willing to donate the technology and funds for these recordings. We've now done five compact disks from our center. The one we did with Count Basie and the New York Voices won a Grammy in 1996. Our name was in every major newspaper in the country. I'd like to build this into a $50-million, high-tech recording company and become the next independent jazz label in the United States.

In addition to the music business, we have a for-profit food-service company. It will generate funds for both Bidwell and Manchester. We are doing about a million dollars right now and should net nearly $100,000 this year. Our mission is to obtain food contracts with entities like hospitals, schools, cultural institutions, and so on. I want to become a $50-million food company over the next ten years. We've also launched a new real-estate division and are building an office tower next door. So we are starting to produce our own revenue. I'm proud of the fact that we have positive cash flow and no operating deficit in any of our units.

The most exciting thing by far, however, is that the program is working. These kids are beginning to see themselves as people with assets and possibilities rather than liabilities and limitations. We're also seeing black kids and white kids going to school together without me giving a civil rights speech to anybody. They're beating each other up in the public schools, but they get along fine here. We have a multimillion-dollar training center in the middle of a poor neighborhood with one of the highest crime rates in Pittsburgh. Yet our building is safe; we have no cameras or security guards on the property.

I could give you a hundred examples of lives that have changed here. Gabriel Tait sluffed out of public school and hung around the Guild. He showed a real knack for photography, so we put him in our program when he was in the sixth grade. He caught fire and went on to Slippery Rock University. He's now working as a staff photographer for the *Detroit Free Press*. Sharif Bey is another one. He was a very troubled kid who wouldn't talk to anybody when he first came here. He came alive in the art studio and also went on to

Slippery Rock. He's now finishing his master's degree in ceramic art and doing a sabbatical in Europe. Here's an inner-city kid who's becoming one of America's young ceramic artists. The experience has transformed his life.

My advice to aspiring social entrepreneurs: First, you've got to have a clear picture of where you want to go. It has to be a vision of the future, not of the past. Then you have to get after it with both feet, full-time. It has to be a full-court press to the future. Number two, you have to develop basic management skills. I'm running a large corporation that could double in size over the next few years. You can't get there from here unless you manage effectively. Poor management will put you out of business quickly—that's just the way it is. Number three, you've got to surround yourself with people who are at least as bright as you, maybe even brighter, then turn 'em loose. Strong teamwork is critical in this profession. Use volunteers everywhere you can, but don't rely on them to run your organization—when they wake up with a head cold or their kids are screaming, they aren't going to feel very charitable. My team gets up whether they feel charitable or not, 'cause I pay 'em. They're in here every day doing a great job. Number four, you've got to create a culture that is progressive and always moving forward. Never be satisfied with where you are; always try to improve on what you have. And number five, take care of yourself so you survive the thing you create. Don't become a derelict who uses drugs and alcohol, then falls apart as a result of creating your enterprise. Keep in good physical and mental health. Be the kind of person others will want to follow into this profession, not run away from. If you do these things, you can make a big difference.

STEDMAN GRAHAM

In 1985, Stedman Graham founded Athletes Against Drugs to give young Chicago students positive alternatives to the drug scene. Stedman enlisted star athletes like Michael Jordan and others to serve as role models for staying drug free and making good life choices. Today, Athletes Against Drugs has helped more than 15,000 youth through drug-prevention education, sports clinics, career mentoring, and scholarship programs. "When young people have these powerful alternatives in their lives," says Stedman, "they are too busy, too motivated, and too self-assured to get dragged into drugs."

I grew up in Whitesboro, New Jersey, a small black town surrounded by a white community. As a youngster, I felt that because of the color of my skin, I couldn't achieve my dreams. Sports became my way out. Playing basketball especially gave me self-esteem, self-discipline, and exposure outside my community. Without sports, I would never have gone to college. Basketball got me a scholarship to Hardin-Simmons University in Abilene, Texas, where I was one of the top scorers and co-captain of the team. After college, I served with the U.S. Army in Germany, where I earned a master's degree in education and played in the European professional basketball league.

After military service, I worked my way up through the Federal Department of Corrections and became the director of education for the Metropolitan Correctional Institution in Chicago. At that time in the early '80s, a lot of athletes were getting into trouble with drugs and making big headlines. They had a negative effect on the young people who were looking up to them, and it seemed to me that these "bad apples" were tainting the whole athletic industry. I thought, "When I was a kid, I looked up to guys like Wilt Chamberlain, Wally Jones, and Luke Jackson. Wouldn't it be great to create an organization of athletes who want to speak out against drugs and encourage young people to make good choices about their lives!" I thought about such an organization for a long time; I just couldn't get it off my mind.

During this same period, I was supplementing my regular income by doing commercial television work. In one of the commercials I did, I was a stand-in double for Michael Jordan. One day in the trailer, I told Michael about my concept for Athletes Against Drugs and asked if he'd support it. He signed up right there as the very first member athlete. That was in October 1985.

Early on, we really didn't have a clear mission other than to keep young people off drugs. We didn't know how to do that effectively, but we held rallies and spoke to youth wherever we could find a forum. We worked with other organizations that had the same focus. We also developed a strong cadre of volunteer athletes from all sports who wanted to positively impact young people: Walter Payton, Chris Evert, Scott Hamilton, Bruce Jenner, Ernie Banks, Jackie Joyner-Kersee.

It took us awhile to create our own internal program. Just like any new organization, we went through some growing pains. Eventually, with input from teachers, parents and health professionals, we created curriculum materials for our classroom Drug Prevention Program. In 1991, in partnership with Chicago schools and youth organizations, we piloted this program in eleven schools for children in the fourth through sixth grades. The program was a big success and has continued to grow. What we do is provide teachers with workbooks and all the supporting materials they need to make lessons on drug prevention fun for youth. The teachers love it because they know the dangers of drugs and how important it is to teach prevention at an early age. Two-thirds of our schoolchildren will use an illicit substance before they turn eighteen. We're not talking about drugs that are harmless; we're talking about drugs that can destroy people's lives. Family background, economics, and skin color don't matter; young people who get involved in drugs have serious problems.

Over the years, we've added other highly successful programs. The most comprehensive is our Fitness and Career Awareness Program. What we try to do here is impact young people's lives holistically. We strive to expand their understanding of who they are and the potential they have in life. These youth get to participate in sports clinics where guest athletes and coaches help them with their athletic skills and sportsmanship. Along the way, we build their self-esteem, reinforce positive health habits, and stress the dangers of substance abuse. They also get to attend role-model presentations where well-known athletes emphasize goal-setting and education. In addition, we teach parents how to reinforce these same concepts in the home.

The career component is an important piece of this program. Many of our youth have never been exposed to a variety of professions and organizations. They can read about the world of work, but seeing it, feeling it, and touching it make a big difference. We actually take them to work settings in different corporations so they can see the connection between their current education and future careers. Young people who have never been in a corporation before get an emotional charge from seeing a nice building and projecting themselves into an environment different from their current circumstances. It really expands their vision and raises their goals. A study done on this program showed that 85 percent of the children who participated decided not to use drugs, 80 percent saw the connection between school and work, and 72 percent learned more about different jobs.

Another program I'm real proud of is called College PREP. We designed this initiative to secure scholarship money for secondary student-athletes not typically recruited by the big-name schools. These are students much like me who would probably not go to college without this support. But the program is more than just going to college. We teach these young adults how to speak, how to present themselves, and we require them to give service back to their communities. So it's really a leadership development program. We are currently operating in forty-one states. Our goal this year is to arrange scholarships for 400 student-athletes.

As to why we've been so successful over the past fifteen years, I think Michael Jordan says it best: "We're not just telling kids to say no to drugs. We're giving them something to say yes to—healthy activities, life skills, youth leadership, and a chance for productive futures." Since 1991, 15,000 students in the Chicago public schools have completed our program—this includes in-class work, sports clinics, field trips, and role modeling. We currently have 2,200 youth enrolled in the program this year. We now have more than 150 professional athletes and Olympic competitors like Pam Shriver, Herschel Walker, Gail Devers, Bonnie Blair, and Warren Moon who participate in Athletes Against Drugs—and we continue to add more names every week.

> More than anything else, our youth seem to appreciate the fact that somebody is paying attention to them.

I think we make a big difference in young people's lives because we care. More than anything else, our youth seem to appreciate the fact that somebody is paying attention to them. The dedication of our staff and 200 volunteers is so encouraging to me. All of us are involved because we believe in what young people can do. Our reward is hearing comments like, "I now want to stay off drugs my whole life," "I learned that drugs mess up your mind," "You taught me to put my education first," "Now I know I can become a star in whatever I do in life." Our sponsors, volunteers, teachers, and young people are all proud to be part of Athletes Against Drugs.

I've learned a lot from starting my own nonprofit organization. First and foremost, you really have to believe in your mission. In this business, passion empowers you to work long hours, and personal commitment helps you last. If you listen to the naysayers who tell you you're crazy, you won't survive. Being passionate about your mission helps you break through all the barriers that arise. You also have to build a strong team of partners who believe in the same things.

Number two, you need a clear strategy for raising money. A nonprofit organization's longevity is based on funding, just like any other business. It's not that easy to raise money anymore because there's a lot of competition out there. So create a business plan that outlines where your funds are going to come from; then use your money wisely. We've developed all kinds of methods for raising funds. We've been supported by the Kellogg Foundation for the past six years. We also raise a lot of money from special events that corporations sponsor. We host a golf tournament every year and are starting fund-raising luncheons that cater to the sports industry. So we do it all.

A third key is to partner up with organizations that already have the infrastructure in place so you don't have to spend all your time and money in operations. We're expanding into six cities across the country right now, but we aren't spending a lot of money on buildings, staff, and operations. Instead, we are integrating our program into existing infrastructures. For example, we hope to be the drug-prevention component for Boys and Girls Clubs and YMCAs across the country. So let the program be the catalyst for building your organization. If the program doesn't work, then your organization is never going to work.

Finally, you have to run a nonprofit organization the same way you run a for-profit business. You need strong accounting, financial, and legal services to keep you out of trouble. Starting the organization isn't the challenge—it's staying in business. You really have to implement sound practices to stay alive. One of these practices is excellent customer service. In a nonprofit organization, that means understanding the people you are trying to serve, then honing your skills and programs to meet their needs. Ask them for ongoing feedback and constantly make changes to serve them better. Keep learning new and different ways of doing things.

Athletes Against Drugs has helped give my life purpose. It has involved me in other community organizations such as Junior Achievement, Hull House, and the Urban League, where I was a trustee. Just as important are the many relationships I've established that have improved the quality of my life. In my upcoming book, I talk about the importance of being so involved in community service that it becomes the thing you do first. You know, people talk about getting involved in business, creating employment opportunities, and making money. But in the end, they realize that the most important thing they can do is to serve. To me, service is the greatest of all virtues and something we all can share. I remember hearing Dr. Martin Luther King say that anybody can be great because anybody can serve. Giving money is fine, but when you serve, you give of your time, which is a perishable resource—that's why it's so precious.

MEREDITH BLAKE

Meredith Blake is the founder of Break the Cycle, an organization that offers prevention programs, legal services, and support to adolescents who are victims of domestic and dating violence. She has created a curriculum used in schools across the country to teach young people how to get out and stay out of unhealthy relationships. In particular, the program educates youth about the law as it pertains to domestic violence. "If we can just help these kids early enough, we won't ever see them as clients in the future," Meredith says. Her passion for this work comes from her own experiences as a teenager. She explains:

I decided to practice public-interest law and prevent domestic violence for a variety of reasons. When I was fourteen, my first boyfriend was verbally and emotionally abusive, and I blamed myself for not knowing how to be a good girlfriend. My family really emphasized solving your own problems, and I felt I was responsible for the success of the relationship. When he became physically abusive, I got out, but I chalked it up as my fault. Since I'd never heard the expression "domestic violence," I didn't equate my experience with any larger societal issue.

Years later when I was doing my undergraduate work at Berkeley, I heard a lot of similar stories from peers about abusive relationships. This opened my eyes to the fact that this issue wasn't just particular to me—it was much larger. So I became active in women's and children's issues and programs. During that time, I really began to understand the dynamics of domestic violence and decided to become a lawyer who served women and children.

When I entered law school, I never intended to start my own nonprofit organization. It just happened that every summer I worked at an organization that dealt with domestic violence and women's health issues, and I got involved in writing and publishing articles on the topic. Probably my biggest eye-opener was working at the legal aid foundation's restraining-order clinic. I would ask the clients I worked with, "When did the abuse begin?" A lot of them would answer, "Do you mean in this relationship or the first time it happened to me?" This underscored the reality that many of these women had been experiencing abuse for a lifetime, and that it started much earlier than most organizations realized. I felt good about the work I was doing, but I was frustrated because it was reactive work.

As I looked for more proactive opportunities to work with youth, I saw that existing programs helped adults and young children affected by violence in the home. These programs had totally ignored junior-high and high-school kids, many of whom were just starting to date and bring violent behaviors learned at home into their first relationships. It makes sense that dating violence begins when dating does. So I saw a whole population of young people who weren't receiving either preventive or intervention services for something they were experiencing at an alarming rate. I really felt strongly that if we wanted to address this issue, we couldn't wait until they were thirty, forty, or fifty years old.

During my last year of law school, I became more and more frustrated that organizations were not helping our youth. I'd worked hard to gain my legal skills and knew they could best be used if I started an organization to prevent kids from becoming involved in domestic violence and provide early assistance to those who were already impacted. I asked a professor I was close to, "Is this crazy for me to go out there and start my own nonprofit organization?" She kind of laughed at me and said, "Yeah, it's absolutely crazy. It's a lot of hard work and sacrifice, but you'll get more out of doing it than anything else in your life. I'm here for you all the way." She had started her own nonprofit years before and knew exactly what I'd be getting myself into.

Once I decided to go for it, I spent what free time I had shaping the idea. I talked with agencies doing domestic violence work with adults, and I talked with kids to see what they were experiencing. I also talked with organizations that had successful legal services, marketing, and fund-raising because I knew I had to acquire business skills. Passion, drive, and energy were great, but they weren't enough. A lot of people told me, "Well, a nonprofit is different from a corporation." And I'm thinking, "Wait a minute! It's still a business and has to be run as such." I had great entrepreneurial spirit, but I didn't have any formal management training. So besides getting invaluable information from successful people, I took courses at the local Center for Nonprofit Management. I also read everything I could get my hands on.

From the beginning I concentrated on building relationships with people who could help. Each time I met with someone, I made it a rule to get three additional names of others who might be interested. I told each person, "Look this is a start-up venture. Right now the whole thing is just me; I have no materials, staff, or office space. If you join me, you'll really need to roll up your sleeves and work."

That scared a lot of people away, but it helped me find a core group of committed people who are still involved today. I started off with three board members, the minimum required to incorporate.

In addition to recruiting a board, I immediately started setting up a cross-disciplinary advisory committee of teachers, lawyers, doctors, and social workers. Domestic violence cuts across so many disciplines, and I knew my legal expertise wasn't enough. I needed all kinds of professionals to bring this vision to life. I asked everyone I met, "Do you know anybody who works with adolescent medicine?" "Do you know someone who's a great teacher?" Because of that, I was able to recruit the director of adolescent medicine at UCLA, as well as a health educator who had taught high school for fifteen years and was admired for her work.

> From the beginning I concentrated on building relationships with people who could help. Each time I met with someone, I made it a rule to get three additional names of others who might be interested.

Meanwhile, I finished law school and took a little time off to take the bar. [Laughs.] Thankfully, I passed. Obviously, I needed the credibility to run a legal-services program. During this time, we ran the organization out of my apartment. We had no money and I wasn't getting paid. [Laughs.] We quickly realized we needed a formal office to secure any serious funding. So my board members and I launched a grassroots funding campaign. I drafted a letter to everyone I had known since I began walking. [Laughs.] I told them what I was doing and asked for their help. We raised almost $30,000 and got an office and some equipment. Once we did that, I started applying for foundation and grant funding. We were successful early on because donors liked our proactive approach with youth.

From the beginning, I had a very clear vision for the organization. First, I wanted to provide the same type of legal services to adolescents in abusive situations that adults receive. Second, I wanted to develop long-term support systems to help these youth

transition from victim to survivor. Third, and perhaps most important, I wanted to offer preventive education to help break the cycle
so we wouldn't see these kids as clients in the future.

With those objectives in mind, we began designing a program
for schools and juvenile facilities. As I talked with students, I was
shocked to learn that even the ones who recognized violent behaviors didn't classify them as illegal. Many didn't know they even had
rights if they were abused, and some felt they had to go through
their parents to get help. So we wanted our program to clearly convey that violent behaviors are crimes with consequences, crimes that
no one at any age has to tolerate.

We created the curriculum with the help of our advisory committee, student interns, and health teacher, who was instrumental
in making high-level material understandable and fun for kids.
When the program was ready to pilot, we launched it in several high
schools and a number of community-based organizations, like the
Boys and Girls Clubs. The response was fabulous! The kids loved the
content because the curriculum is so interactive. Every school we
visited invited us back and referred us to other schools. So from that
beginning, things really took off.

We've continued to revamp the program based on our observations and feedback from the kids. Today, it consists of three one-
hour segments of video, discussion, and role-playing. The program
is taught by a staff attorney with additional assistance from pro-
bono attorneys from the community. The kids explore a hypotheti-
cal case study of Robert and Lisa over three days. Day one is
Domestic Violence 101, where they learn the differences between
physical, verbal, emotional, and sexual abuse. We talk about the
cycle of violence and patterns of control. We address topics like:
Why is it difficult for kids to get out of these relationships? What are
the obstacles to getting help?

On day two we talk about the crimes commonly associated with
domestic violence. We actually define and give examples of assault

and battery, stalking, and date rape. We discuss questions like: What are your rights? What is a restraining order? How do you get one?

Then on day three we hold a mock hearing for a restraining order. The kids actually play the roles of Robert and Lisa, the witnesses, the bailiff, and the court reporter. The kids really love it because they learn so much and teach each other in the process.

Along with the education, we provide free legal services and advocacy. When we are in the schools, inevitably a number of kids say, "What you're talking about is exactly what's happening in my home" or "That's what's going on in my relationship." We help these kids get temporary restraining orders and actually represent them at hearings for permanent orders. We also have an advocacy program that helps parents and teachers enforce these orders and keep the kids safe. This youth population presents different challenges than the adult population. For example, with adults, you craft restraining orders to keep the abuser a hundred yards away from the home or the workplace. With kids, the abuser may be sitting three seats away in English class. So our program teaches schools how to deal with the repercussions that arise when both students are on campus.

We've now been in dozens of schools and community-based organizations. We also teach at the boys' and girls' units at juvenile hall. Our program director, who is an attorney, used to teach between 400 and 500 students a month. As the demand kept increasing, we decided to teach a core of local attorneys how to deliver the program. We now hold quarterly training sessions for them, which increases substantially the number of students we can reach each year. In addition, we're beginning a strategic planning process for expanding our services nationally.

Of course, it costs money to provide these services. About half of our funding comes from individual donors and special events; the other half comes from private foundations. Right now, I'm working hard to find regular income streams that are dependable.

I'm concentrating on cause-related marketing and corporate partnerships. For example, I just launched an initiative called Take a Firm Stand Against Domestic Violence. What we are trying to do is get law firms to commit to long-term support. We're also trying to find corporations that want to reach our youth population as either customers or employees. We are a prime partner for The Gaps of the world, as well as stores that sell health and beauty products. So we're asking ourselves: What businesses are trying to sell to our constituency? How can we both benefit from collaboration? These are our most important funding questions today.

If you want to be successful in the nonprofit world, you need to learn how to run a business. You need to manage your operation the same way you would a for-profit company. Educate yourself in accounting, business management, human resources, legal services, and marketing. These are your survival skills in this competitive world.

Second, you can't do it alone. Even though you can't always pay people to be on your team, you can appeal to their interests and passions. And don't look for people just like you. Find partners who have strengths that compensate for your weaknesses. Then your team will be strong and complete.

Third, and something I haven't been very successful at [laughs], try to keep a balance in your life, because a nonprofit organization can take over twenty-four hours a day, seven days a week. People warned me about this, but I didn't believe it. You also find yourself with a lot of blurred lines. I mean, everybody in my personal life is also involved in my work life. It's a compliment that they want to be that involved, but to really stay healthy, you've got to find things to sustain yourself outside of work. That's one of my goals this year.

One final thought: I think that volunteerism has surged because our view of how to change the world has changed. In the '60s, people felt a great deal of frustration and anger and had a passion for social justice. But they weren't necessarily planning far enough into the future, and consequently many of that decade's efforts weren't sustainable. This new generation has an eye for long-term strategic planning. I don't agree with the Generation X designation as a group of apathetic couch potatoes. My organization is really powered by young adults who want to make the world better. We now have eleven volunteers on our board, twelve on our advisory committee, and many more who work in our auxiliary groups. We also have dozens and dozens of people who just call and do everything from fund-raising to awareness raising. Many of these are the middle- and high-school students we are teaching. All these volunteers have come on board to help break the cycle of domestic violence. And everyone who gets involved soon discovers that this kind of work gives you something that nothing else can—the fulfillment that comes from making life better for your friends, your neighbors, your family, your children, and yourself.

BILL HALAMANDARIS

Bill Halamandaris is the founder of The Heart of America, an organization that seeks out great role models and links them up with schools in an effort to inspire youth to get involved in serving their communities. Kids who participate are rewarded with money for college. As a result, they are able to further their own position in life and, in turn, go out as ambassadors to inspire yet others. Here's Bill's story:

My father was part of the depression generation. He desperately wanted an education, but circumstances did not allow it. He took the only job he could find, which was in a coal mine. As a result, he got emphysema. When I was thirteen years old, he came home one day, told me this news, and made me promise I would somehow get an education. Frankly, that was the most difficult thing I ever had to do. Everything else in life has been relatively easy.

I was fortunate enough to get a scholarship to George

Washington University. I went on to law school. I loved what the law stood for but realized its application had more to do with presentation skills than justice. So I started looking for a more useful way to spend my life. After a period of self-analysis, I found myself doing investigations for the United States Senate. I went through the ranks of investigator, chief investigator, counsel, and staff director of the committees that do oversight for Congress. I think we did a pretty good job figuring out what was going wrong and ways to be more efficient, but I kept seeing things reoccur. You know, the problem we'd solve today would reappear in two years in a different guise. I used to call it the waterbed principle. You press down here and it pops up over there. I started feeling that most problems are too big for government, and that we need to find ways to rally everyone to do their part.

The real issue here is how to get back to where we began. How do we help people understand that together we can solve all of our problems. Tocqueville discussed this at length. He said the most remarkable thing about our society is the way we band together whenever a problem appears. Someone decides to do something, other people join in, and before long we have a group solving the problem. This is the essence of America and the reason for our success as a nation. As Tocqueville suggested, "America is great because America is good. And America will cease to be great when it is no longer good." When we get distracted by our egos, materialism, and other superficial things, we do ourselves and society a great disservice.

The problem I had with my role in Congress is that we spent most of our time turning over rocks, focusing on little masses of people who were not very appealing. We would put the spotlight on them, and they would seem to disappear. This philosophy says you make a difference by stopping people from being bad. The focus is on negative things, on people who are less than admirable. This is also the philosophy espoused by the media. Negative stories are easy to tell; they are quick in and quick out. Unfortunately, they end up constructing our reality in society.

A more productive philosophy is to accentuate the positive. You seek out the best people you can find and give them visibility. The goal is to create an ever-increasing spiral of inspiration. That's the thing that is most appealing to me about the nonprofit sector. The only reason we exist is to save or change lives. If a nonprofit organization responds to needs and is constructed on the right values, it can make a huge difference in the community. The people who lead this effort are our true heroes, our true problem-solvers. For every significant problem I hear about in the media right now, I know some human being who is doing something significant to solve it. And that's very inspiring to me.

This second philosophy was the foundation of our first organization, the Caring Institute, which we started in 1985. Our design was pure and simple: to find the best examples we could and elevate their visibility in the community. There is so much negativity in our world that we felt people desperately needed positive role models, particularly our kids. Albert Schweitzer, who is one of my heroes, once said, "Example isn't the best way to teach; it's the only way." So we sought out great role models, honored them, wrote about them, and hoped other people would want to be like them.

After doing this for a while, we decided to take the next step and start The Heart of America. Our main objective was to replicate these incredible role models. Most of the people who helped me start the organization have been honored by the Caring Awards, the Jefferson Awards, the Point of Light Awards, or other national awards. We talked at length about how to replicate their number. The consensus we reached was to focus on kids and values. These are the most precious things we have in America.

The first stage of our program is to send extraordinary role models into the community as our ambassadors. To be honest with you, it's a model of discipleship. We find the best people we can, put them in front of audiences, and hope they will inspire others to become like them. The goal is to create a geometric progression of inspiration and service. Right now we have two groups of speakers: young people, who typically speak to their peers in the schools; and adults, who typically speak to professional and civic audiences. We try to match the right speaker with the right audience.

The next stage is to recruit second-generation ambassadors from the audiences we visit. Today was a good example. We had two young people speak at an elementary school in Anacostia, one of the poorest areas in Washington, D.C. They both happen to be African-Americans who have pulled themselves out of difficult circumstances. They tell their stories and conclude with, "If I can do it, you can do it." Then we encourage the kids to make some contribution to their school or community. We try to help them understand that we are all in this together, and that we help ourselves when we help others.

The third stage of the process is to identify those students who are willing to make a commitment to serve. Then we go out into the community and find sponsors who are willing to respond to the challenge. In other words, if the kids are willing to help the community, the community must be willing to reward the kids. What we do is ask the sponsor to put three dollars into a bank account in the kid's name for every hour the kid serves in the community. The money is then available to further that student's education. It can be used for trade school, vocational school, junior college, university, or whatever. So these students are building sweat equity in their own future. As a thirteen-year-old kid, I would have loved a program like this. I would have said, "I may not be smart enough to get a scholarship, but here's something I can do. I can further my education by serving my community."

The need for this program is huge, especially in our inner-city schools. I went to the school in Anacostia today with our two speakers and asked the kids some questions. I said, "How many of you know someone who is in jail?" Out of 400 kids, guess how many hands went up? All of them! Next I asked, "How many of you know someone who is doing drugs?" Again, all the hands went up. Then I asked, "How many of you know someone who has been to college?" At that point, we were down to about 25 percent of the kids. Finally, I said, "How many of you know an executive, bank president, or someone with a prominent role in the community?" Now we were down to about 10 percent of the kids.

All the evil alternatives you can imagine are readily available to these kids. I mean, you don't have to be smart or talented to sell drugs, steal a car, or break into a house. You can do these things no matter what your circumstances. Conversely, the only way these kids can advance themselves in a positive way is to have extraordinary talent: they have to be able to run real fast, hit a ball real hard, shoot baskets real well, or do something else that pays off financially. Short of this, there is no broadly available mechanism for these kids to climb out of difficult circumstances. Our program provides a positive way out. It allows average students to serve their communities and advance themselves in the process. That's the genius of our design.

And the community has responded. It's not a tough sell because it's a win-win situation. Everyone involved benefits: the kid, the family, the sponsor, the educational system, and the community. It's a great bang for a buck because each dollar invested is multiplied in many ways. Our sponsors are pretty enthusiastic about the program. Here's a good example: A gentleman in Indianapolis named Don Palmer contacted us and said, "I like what you are doing. Let me sponsor some schools here in Indianapolis." So we identified four schools where 75 percent of the students were below the poverty line. We thought these schools could generate 10,000 hours of service to the community, and Don made the financial commitment. Well, after a few months we had 20,000 hours of service committed from these schools. So we said, "Okay, guys, the students are really responding. What are we going to do about this?" Don told a friend of his, who said, "I'll pick up some of the difference." Then I told a friend of mine, who said, "I'll pick up the rest." So sponsors are stepping forward.

The best way to summarize our program is with the four Rs: Recruit, Recruit, Reward, Recognize. We first *recruit* great role models to serve as ambassadors. These people then *recruit* second-generation role models to expand the army. Next, we *reward* people financially for doing positive things in their community. Finally, we *recognize* them in various ways in an attempt to inspire others to get involved. Right now we have adult role models in forty-two states and youth role models in twenty-six states. We have a professional speakers' bureau called Speaking From the Heart that books our adult speakers. We also run the school programs out of our office, although some of the young people have taken the bit between their teeth and organized local chapters. It's hard to quantify how many people we reach each year, but in the three-state area around here, we made 111 presentations last year. This reached 15,000 students in this area alone.

The way we fund our organization has been kind of miraculous. When we first got started, the people involved were so enthusiastic they agreed to provide the seed money. These were individuals and corporations, some in the world of charity and some in the world of business. Since then, they have agreed to fund our administrative costs in perpetuity. So we don't do any corporate fund-raising: we don't write grants, we don't take money from the government, we don't do direct-mail marketing. Pure and simple, we focus on our mission. The money we get from our sponsors goes 100 percent to the kids. And it's multiplied ten times over before it reaches fruition. We simply tell our story and welcome people to our "family" if they want to help. But it's a call of the heart; we don't talk anyone into doing anything.

It's interesting that most of the people in our family, though now in privileged circumstances, have had severe obstacles to overcome. I mean, nobody gets through life unscarred; we all have stories to tell. A lot of people ask, "Why do we have to suffer?" "Why do we have to hurt?" "Why do bad things happen?" I think we go through these experiences to benefit others. If we pass on each lesson we learn, we complete the cycle. To me, there is nothing more tragic than someone with tremendous experiences and resources who chooses not to share those gifts. I can't imagine facing my Maker and having him say, "I gave you all of these things to work with, but you did nothing with them."

> To me, there is nothing more tragic than someone with tremendous experiences and resources who chooses not to share those gifts.

What we're trying to teach these kids is to use whatever gifts they've been given, regardless of their circumstances. We want them to know that when you help other people, you also help yourself. We always try to practice what we preach. While talking with the principal in Anacostia to arrange our speakers today, we learned that the vast majority of kids at the school would not be getting a Christmas present. Our response was, "We can't solve all the problems in the world, but we can do something about this one." So we hit the toy stores last night, shopped until one in the morning, and bought 400 toys—one for every child in that school. We stayed up late wrapping them, then delivered them this morning. And you know who got the most out of that process? The kids all got a toy, but we'll never forget the surprise and delight of 400 children who never dreamed they would get a Christmas present from a group of strangers. It was really quite remarkable!

Most of the people in our organization are heavily involved in community service. Let me tell you a story about Melissa Poe, one of our ambassadors. At the age of seven, Melissa was watching a program called "Highway to Heaven." The episode was all about our environment. They were predicting what the world would be like in the year 2010, or something like that. Melissa decided she didn't want to live in a world like that. So she did what any seven-year-old would do. She wrote a letter to the biggest adult she could find—the president of the United States. She got an unresponsive form letter back. What is significant here is not the government's response but Melissa's response. She could have gone out to play. She could have just blown it off. She could have said, "If the president won't help, what can I do?" Instead, she decided to tackle the problem herself.

She went down to a billboard company and asked how much a billboard cost. The guy gave her a number. Then she said, "I don't want any old billboard, I want a really good one." So he gave her another number. She didn't tell him what it was for at that point. She came back three months later, after doing all the things kids do to make money—lemonade stands, pop bottles—plunked this bag of quarters down, and said, "I want that billboard." The guy says, "What are you going to do with it?" She told him she wanted to put a message up there about taking care of the environment. Well, the guy was so impressed that he gave her the billboard for free. I'm sure you could see that coming. What grew out of that was a national billboard campaign Melissa organized. When I met her, she was presiding over an international club of 400,000 kids who were all involved in protecting the environment—it's called Kids' Face. The next year, she was the youngest person to address the summit on the environment. And, of course, she was standing next to the president.

You probably never heard about Melissa until I told you this story, even though she's one of our more celebrated young people. The sad thing is, if she had taken her dad's handgun to school, it would have been in all the papers, on all the newscasts, and everyone would know about it. So which event is more remarkable? Which one should we honor and celebrate? Which one is most important? Is it a single act of destruction or a commitment to solve a problem and lift people up? Our society's preoccupation with negative events is what we're trying to counteract at The Heart of America.

I think the number-one key to success for a nonprofit organization is integrity. You have to stay focused on your mission; you have to do what you say you are going to do; and you have to do it for the right reason. There is a world of difference between doing the right thing and doing the right thing for the right reason. A lot of charities get into trouble because they gradually evolve from giving to taking. That's the surest way to fail in the long run.

The second thing is, you have to surround yourself with an army of committed people. You can't be the only one carrying the flag. It's interesting to me that the top answer on every survey on why people volunteer is, "Somebody asked me." I find that a lot of people want to help but don't feel they can make a difference. Once they get involved, they experience the joy of giving and realize they do have an impact. The truth is, we all make a difference, even if it's just by our existence. When we realize that we change the world just by being here, we start thinking differently. We start saying, "I can affect this situation. I can change the outcome. I can influence people, even if it's just with a smile." I think it's our birthright to change the world, and all of us need to participate. That's my message.

CHAPTER · 4

HEALING OUR AFFLICTED

Your body is precious. It is our vehicle for awakening. Treat it with care.

BUDDHA

They that be whole need not a physician, but they that are sick.

MATTHEW 9:12

The Lord will maintain the cause of the afflicted, and the right of the poor.

PSALM 140:12

Robert Rocha was one troubled fellow. During his childhood, his mother was in and out of jail for robbing banks, so he was put in foster care at the age of eight. A few years later, he was using heroin, selling drugs, and sleeping wherever he could. He carried a gun to pull holdups and a knife to stab people—which he did. While still a juvenile, he was arrested and charged with twenty-seven counts of armed robbery.

At age nineteen, Robert was sent to San Quentin. Of his experience he says, "I'd lost touch with everything and had no belief in myself. No hope. No trust in nothing or nobody. The reason I wanted to go to prison was because that's where I could be somebody. But when I got there, nothing in prison excited me, because I'd done everything by then. When I got back out on the street, I thought about changing my life. Then I got busted again for selling heroin to an undercover cop."

As a last-ditch effort to save his life, Robert entered the Delancey Street program in San Francisco, an organization run by Mimi Silbert. Barely five feet tall and around a hundred pounds, Mimi can hold her ground with the hardest criminals in America. One day while Robert and other Delancey Street residents were building a new complex, she said, "You want to quit? Well, that's what you've always done—given up every time it has gotten difficult! I know you are hammering away and thinking that this isn't worth it, but you're hammering away on your lives. You're building your own foundation. If you make a mistake with that wall, tear it down and rebuild it! That's what we are doing at Delancey Street, for ourselves—tearing down bad things and making good things to replace 'em. And if you're too guilty and angry and hopeless to fight for yourself, then do it for the next guy. Because he's counting on you."

The message eventually got through to Robert; he realized he did care about himself and other people—and the realization brought him to tears. During the next few years at Delancey Street, Robert totally transformed his life against all odds. He learned eight construction trades, took courses in criminology, taught geometry, and helped other ex-convicts earn high-school diplomas. Today, Robert is confident and successful. He is one of thousands of men and women—once afflicted by drugs, crime, and violence—who are now teachers, attorneys, construction workers, and business people—thanks to Mimi Silbert and the Delancey Street Foundation.

Millions of Americans suffer from drug and alcohol addictions, physical disabilities, mental retardation, and emotional illnesses. This is an area where big-hearted people can make a real contribution. Here are some of our challenges.

Alcohol and drug abuse affect approximately 20 percent of our adult population during any given year. One million Americans are currently being treated for alcohol and drug addictions in more than 10,000 facilities across the country. Alcohol, in particular, can harm every organ and system of the body. It is the single most important cause of liver disease; it is associated with cardiovascular disease; and it contributes to approximately 65 percent of all cases of pancreatitis. Nearly one-fourth of all patients admitted to general hospitals have problems with alcohol and are being treated for the consequences of their drinking. In addition, alcohol contributes to 100,000 deaths annually, making it the third leading cause of preventable mortality in the United States, behind tobacco and unhealthy patterns of diet and inactivity.

Along with various addictions, forty million adults and twelve million children are affected by mental illness. It is estimated that one-third of all Americans will suffer with some form of mental illness at some point in their lives. In addition, over seven million people in our country have mental retardation. More than 100,000 newborn babies are added to that number annually. Research now shows a clear relationship between mental retardation and poverty. Malnutrition, lead poisoning, and lack of prenatal care are a few of the contributing factors. Other causes of mental retardation are substance abuse, rubella, meningitis, and chromosome abnormalities.

Physical illnesses are also a challenge for many people. More than a million new cases of cancer are diagnosed each year. Breast cancer alone will affect more than 170,000 women this year, and more than 40,000 will die. It is estimated that over a ten-year period, nearly two million women will be diagnosed with breast cancer; the majority of these women will have no risk factors. Statistics suggest that 30 percent of all Americans will suffer from some form of cancer during their lifetime. In addition, one out of five adolescents has a chronic illness or physical disability such as asthma, diabetes, cerebral palsy, cystic fibrosis, or paraplegia. While these conditions generally do not affect cognitive ability, they do impair the person's ability to work and be productive.

The stories that follow show how much difference one person can make. Pedro Greer started the Camillus Health Concern to provide state-of-the-art medical care to the poor and homeless in Miami. Nancy Brinker created the Susan G. Komen Breast Cancer Foundation to help fund breast-cancer research and education. Anthony Shriver launched Best Buddies International to provide friendship and life mentoring to people with mental retardation. Mimi Silbert started Delancey Street to free people from drug and alcohol addictions and criminal behavior. And Patience White created the Adolescent Employment Readiness Center to help young people with physical disabilities and chronic illnesses develop career skills and learn to provide for themselves. These are the role models we should be talking about in America.

PEDRO GREER

Pedro Greer is a legend in Miami. He is the founder of the Camillus Health Concern, a health-care clinic that serves the poor and homeless. He and his team of volunteer physicians treat more than 10,000 patients each year, free of charge. Pedro established the first medical-school classes and rotation in a homeless clinic in America. He has won numerous awards for his work, including the MacArthur Fellowship and the Presidential Service Award. Here is his story:

I am a natural-born immigrant. I was born here by mistake. My mother was visiting the United States from Havana in 1956. I was born in the emergency room; then we went back to Cuba. We ended up back in the United States after the revolution. My father always tells me, "We were one of the few families that lost nothing when Fidel Castro took over." I said, "Dad, why did we lose nothing?" He said, "Son, we had nothing, so we lost nothing." [Laughs.]

I went to the University of Florida as an undergrad, then went to medical school in Santiago, Dominican Republic. It was a

European-style school, so my program was six years long. During my fourth year, I planned to meet my sister in Miami to celebrate her birthday. I was going to fly in, and she was going to drive down. Just before I left Santiago, my mother called to tell me my sister had been killed in a car accident. Needless to say, it was devastating for our family. She was the youngest child and the apple of my father's eye. At the time, I made a promise to myself and God that when I became a doctor, I would do all I could to see that people don't have to suffer or die alone. See, medicine's all about taking care of people. I'm a liver specialist, but I have never had a liver walk into my office. It's amazing! There is always a person wrapped around it. [Laughs.]

I came back to Miami in 1984 as an intern at Jackson Memorial Hospital. I planned to finish my training, then go to North Africa or the Caribbean and take care of poor people. I started my rotation in the intensive care unit. One of the first cases I had was a man dying of pulmonary tuberculosis. On his wristband were his name and age, but it said "no address." This meant that fire rescue had found him on the streets and brought him in. It really disturbed me that he was alone, so I went out onto the streets to find his family. I spent four days visiting different shelters but never found them. Unfortunately, he died prior to the end of my rotation, of a disease that is easily preventable. What this experience did was open my eyes to the world of extreme poverty. This was America; poverty was supposed to exist elsewhere. I decided it was not for me to judge these people or their circumstances. By my beliefs, God is the only one who is supposed to judge. I'm a physician, and it's my role take care of people who are sick.

So I decided to start a free clinic for the poor with some other interns. Back then we were young and stupid. As the years have gone by, we're no longer young, but we remain stupid. [Laughs.] We ran

> Medicine's all about taking care of people. I'm a liver specialist, but I have never had a liver walk into my office. There is always a person wrapped around it.

this clinic in a local shelter called the Camillus House. We did it every Tuesday and Thursday after we finished at the hospital. We would bring in an exam table and use the cafeteria as the waiting room. It was all volunteers for four years; they were easy to get. It was fun! It's what you're supposed to do! There are very few people in the health profession that don't want to help. Of course, my brother-in-law, who's a lawyer, kept telling us, "You could get sued, so be careful." I'm thinking, what do I have? Medical-school loans and a mother-in-law. [Laughs.]

We really wanted to help, but we realized that we knew nothing about public health, politics, turf wars, all that stuff. We decided to ask the homeless how we could best help them, so we went out under the bridges in my jeep. We did this to prove that we were trustworthy. One of the first things you're taught in medical school is that 80 percent of your diagnosis can be done with an appropriate history. Now an appropriate history can be done only if the person trusts you enough to tell the truth. So going under the bridges was nothing more than making people feel comfortable enough to come to the clinic. We visited some people for six months before they came in. It was funny because it was Mark O'Connell, Tom and Bill Harrington, and me. Now I'm Cuban-Irish, but my last name is Greer, so we called ourselves the Irish Bridge Team, the IBT. [Laughs.] We spoke both English and Spanish, even though these guys are as Irish as you get. I mean, they're not white, they're fluorescent. [Laughs.] These are the guys that support the sunscreen industry, okay?

So for four years we ran this free clinic with no funding. Then one day I get this funny call; I remember it exactly. The guy on the phone says, "We've been following what you're doing, and we've got two things that will help: some private funding and the McKinney Act through Congress." Well, the private funding ended up being Comic Relief, the HBO show with Whoopie Goldberg—I now sit on their board. The other thing was the McKinney Act that provides funding for the homeless. Alina Perez-Stable, who was a social worker with me at the hospital at the time and is now our administrator, helped me write up the application. Her father was one of my professors and mentors.

What we did was acquire the building next to the shelter; it was a lighting store that had been closed for a while. We got it for a buck a year! My old roommate and best buddy from high school, Carlos Santiero, is a building contractor. He came in and built the entire 7,000-square-foot clinic, under cost and ahead of schedule. Just before we opened up, he calls me and says, "I'm having a little problem with the city. They won't give me a certificate of occupancy unless we redo their sidewalk." I said, "How much will that cost?" He said, "Eight thousand dollars." I said, "Carlos, I think we can operate a clinic without a certificate of occupancy." He said, "As your contractor, I've got to tell you, you can't do that." I said, "Well, thanks for telling me. Just let 'em try to close us down." This is the city of Miami, the fourth-poorest city in America, and they're going to close us down for a sidewalk? So we opened up without the certificate of occupancy. Once a guy from the city called, and I told him, "Come on down. I'll bring all the patients out, including the women and children, and we'll sit on the sidewalk to see how bad it really is. But please tell me when you're coming so I can advise the television stations." [Laughs.] I never heard from them again. We were saving the city millions of dollars, doing their health care for free.

I've got to tell you another funny story. The clinic is a block away from the new arena where the Miami Heat play. One of the city commissioners, who just got out of prison for corruption, wanted the commission to vote on whether or not to arrest the homeless on game nights. I played football in high school and college and am sort of a competitive guy. I said to them, "We just spent sixty million dollars on this arena, and the team is 0 and 17. Let's arrest the coach and leave the homeless alone." [Laughs.] You've got to love this stuff!

When we opened the new clinic, we hired a staff. Our mission is to adhere to the real needs of the patients we are treating. Sometimes the big giant medical centers say, "Come to us, come to the mountain." Well, when you're very poor, uneducated, and lack transportation, there's no way you're going to get there. We learned early on that the medical problems of the poor are secondary to their poverty and social problems. So with our new funding, we hired one doctor and six social workers. Let me tell you two stories that taught me important lessons.

It was Tuesday night, and I'm at the clinic supervising a fourth-year student. He goes in to see a twenty-five-year-old white woman. She was dressed in spandex, with smeared makeup and all that stuff. He comes out and says, "I can't talk to her; she's crying way too much." I'm wondering, is it crack, heroine, cocaine, psychosis, depression? These can all cause severe physical pain. So I walk in there and take her by the arm, and she calms down. It was like doing pediatrics, where you can't get the kid to talk because she's so scared. Well, she was crying because she'd been raped the night before. I asked her why she didn't go to Jackson Memorial Hospital, which has a gazillion beds. She said, "Doc, look how I'm dressed. I couldn't take the comments people would make." So this poor woman took twenty-four hours to come in because of the judgments we make in society. How many other people have been violated out there and don't come in for whatever reason? It reinforced my belief that compassion is the greatest thing we offer in medicine. It doesn't matter what kind of policies we create or systems we build; it comes down to taking care of that individual person. So that always stuck with me.

Here's the other story. It was lunchtime when I got to the clinic. There was a mother there with three young children. Now I want you to picture a couple of things. This is America, where success is measured by your income and position. Living in poverty means you're a failure. It's even worse if you're a kid. Imagine being a homeless child with a mom who has no job or education. The clothes you wear are all donated, and you know how kids are in school. On a good day, you get a shelter dinner. And when you get sick, you come to Camillus, which is a great clinic, but it's for poor folks. I'm trying to set this up so you understand how this child must feel. So I go in there with my lunch bag and give the youngest kid my sandwich—he was probably five or six years old. The kid takes a couple of bites and sticks the sandwich into his pocket. I asked him why he did that. He looks at me sort of surprised and says, "It's for my brothers." Now I have three postdoctoral fellowships, I've been taught by Nobel Laureates, and I'm an assistant dean at the university, and this little homeless child—with the simplest of words and actions—explained to me what we're supposed to be doing. I always think about that child.

Anyway, we were in the 7,000-square-foot building from 1984 until 1998. We had more than 40,000 patient visits last year; our first year we saw 500 patients. In August, we opened a new 18,000-square-foot building. We have the same staff but a lot more volunteers. I am now the assistant dean for Homeless Education at the University of Miami. It's a required course in the medical school, so we have a large pool of volunteers. We have fifty to sixty volunteer nurses and about 200 volunteer physicians, representing all the sub-specialties. When the volunteers go out there, I tell 'em, "Don't feel sorry for these people because they are poor and homeless. If you were poor and homeless, would you want a depressed doctor taking care of you?" [Laughs.] It's actually great for the volunteers. They love it! At one time, we had too many volunteers and not enough patients. It was kind of a comedy. We were yelling out the window, "Please come in; we've got cardiologists in here." [Laughs.] It was the exact opposite of an HMO.

We fund the clinic with grants from private foundations and the federal government. All our equipment is donated by medical-supply companies, and our medicines are donated by pharmaceutical reps. The clinic actually does a lot more than just treat the poor.

We are very aggressive with education and prevention. We've been able to bring down the number of incidents of HIV among the homeless from 24 percent, one of the highest in the country, to 7 percent. Everyone on our staff, including the intake person, who was formerly homeless, is a trained HIV counselor. But you name it, we take care of it: tuberculosis, diabetes, hypertension. We estimate that our actual costs would be nearly $6 million a year if we were buying all the stuff and everyone was getting paid. I continue to work as a volunteer. At first I did it because it's what you're supposed to do. Now I do it because it keeps me out of the politics. It also helps with the negotiations, because I can get 'em with the big guilt stuff. "Hey, we're taking care of poor people. I'm not getting paid either. You're gonna take a profit on this? What, are you crazy?" [Laughs hard.] You know, being six two and a half and 245 pounds also helps. I would never threaten anyone, but it's always nice to stand up. [Laughs.]

I think there are three rules for doing this kind of work. Number one, don't take yourself seriously. The work you do is serious, but don't take yourself seriously. Too many people in the world of social work believe they have a monopoly on the truth. They feel they are destined by God to do a certain thing. I believe God gives us the freedom to do what we want. We are here to help people and should do the best we can, but we get to choose. So don't take yourself too seriously. Do you follow what I'm saying? That's number one.

Number two, understand your limitations. I am a physician; I know health care. But I didn't know health care in impoverished areas. I learned because I was open to my limitations. When you do something like this, you have to be willing to learn. If you think you're this knight in shining armor, it's condescending to the people you are trying to help.

The third rule is, build a team of people with the needed skills. For example, those of us with social passion generally lack business experience. I know that. So what do you do? You go to your buddies who do real well in business and say, "Help me set up a business plan." Then you give credit to everybody who helps. And sometimes you give credit to people who don't deserve it, but you build the team. Remember, you're not out there for yourself. Your first and foremost objective has to be helping your fellow human beings. So find people who can make things happen.

A final thought: To me, the beauty of America is its philosophy. Democracy is a very slow process, and it's not perfect. But you know what? The difference between America and other countries is that we are allowed to, and in many ways obligated to, solve our own problems. And that makes this place special. When people tell me they want to make a difference, I say, "Find something that's a passion in your heart. Do you like the arts? Do the arts. When you take inner-city kids into a museum, you open a window into a world they have never seen. Do you like helping people? Become a doctor." Now, I'm no longer skinny and my hair isn't black, but I love seeing these young students go through this experience. They have brilliant minds, great hearts, and they want to save the world. They are saying, "Something is wrong; let's make it better." It is so inspiring! And that's the great thing about America: There just isn't a darn thing we can't do to make things right!

NANCY BRINKER

Nancy Brinker is the founder of the Susan G. Komen Breast Cancer Foundation. She started the organization as a promise to her sister, Susan, who died of breast cancer at the age of thirty-six. Nancy, herself a victim of the dreaded disease, has built Komen into the nation's largest private funder of breast-cancer research and education. More than 30,000 volunteers help promote activities that now raise $50 million a year. With 700,000 participants, the foundation's flagship event, "Race for the Cure," has become the largest series of 5K fitness runs in the world.

Nancy started this incredible organization in the guest room of her house with a broken typewriter, a couple of hundred dollars, and a shoebox full of friends' names. Here's her story:

My life in volunteerism was really influenced by my family, especially my mother. She comes from a family of incredible doers and taught us that true charity is not just giving, but giving without being asked and without recognition. As young children, she would drag us all over the place in the back of her old station wagon to give service. When we wanted to be slumming with our friends, we'd be going down to work at the YWCA. Wherever she went, we had to go! We learned that where much is given, much is expected. If our mother noticed that we weren't wearing something regularly—a pair of shoes, a sweater, a blouse, a skirt—we would come home and it would be gone. She could always find someone who needed it more. Perhaps most important, she taught my sister and me that this is our country, that we should cherish it and fix things that aren't right. Her watchword to us was always, "You'll never get anything done sitting around on your duff."

Suzy and I became aware of the polio epidemic when she was nine and I was six. We decided we wanted to help, so we organized a polio benefit show in our backyard in Peoria, Illinois. We raised $64, and our mother took us to the Polio Association to give them the check. That was our first entry into the world of charitable giving on our own. I'll never forget the joy I felt that day! Little did I know that twenty-five years later, Suzy and I would be involved in trying to "fix" something else that was terribly wrong—breast cancer.

Suzy was diagnosed with the disease when she was thirty-three years old. At the time, we had no idea this battle would take her life. She was such an incredibly charitable person. Even in her last days, she continued to comfort other cancer patients. She would walk down the hall in her little robe and slippers and talk to children who were being treated. Her last request to me was that, together, we would do something to fight this dreaded disease so other families would not have to suffer the way we had. She could never say she was dying because she was so young. She used to say, "When I get well, Nanny, will you help me do something?" I would always say, "Of course I will." When she died, I realized I had no choice. I had no idea what to do, but I was going to fulfill Suzy's dying wish if it was the last thing I did.

At the time, patients did not have good access to comprehensive cancer centers, the Internet, or toll-free numbers to call for support. There was little awareness of breast cancer and no one organization to fight the disease. When Suzy was diagnosed, approximately one out of eleven women were developing the disease over their lifetime. I was shocked when I learned that 330,000 women died of breast cancer between 1970 and 1980—compared to 59,000 Americans in the Vietnam War. I realized we needed an organization, not just to support patients like Suzy but also to conduct research to prevent and eradicate the disease.

So I started thinking about how to proceed. I had some experience with business and marketing but knew nothing about nonprofit organizations. I really had to learn along the way. In 1982 we officially incorporated as the Susan G. Komen Breast Cancer Foundation. We started off in the guest room of my house with a semibroken typewriter, a shoebox full of friend's names, and a couple hundred dollars I swiped from my grocery fund. I quickly realized that people were afraid of cancer and didn't want to talk about it, especially breast cancer. A lot of women who suffered with the disease never discussed it, and most people had no idea how devastating it was—socially, culturally, emotionally, and especially physically. All the CEOs I approached, both men and women, blushed at the word *breast*. Their attitudes were, "Fund it but don't talk about." So it was not easy getting started.

My husband, Norman Brinker, was a tremendous support in those early days. He is a brilliant businessman and a well-known polo player—he competed in the Olympics when he was younger.

So the first event we did was a lady's outdoor international polo tournament. We thought people might be interested in seeing women do something that was different. Well, the tournament never took place because it rained that day. I remember standing out on the polo field crying, with color running down my hands from the soggy crepe-paper streamers. I was babbling to myself about being a failure because no one would show up in the rain. As I turned around, I saw a stream of cars coming in the driveway with their lights on. It was divine intervention! Everyone turned out because they were intrigued by the cause.

The next year, we held a luncheon that was attended by nearly 800 men and women, including our dear friend Betty Ford, whose speech drew national attention to the foundation. Although the luncheon was a huge success, I realized we needed a major grassroots event to educate millions about this disease and, simultaneously, raise enormous amounts of money. At that time, everybody was running, jumping, and doing aerobics. I envisioned an event where people could come together to run, walk, share survival stories, and sign up for their first mammogram. That's how Race for the Cure began in 1983. And it took a lot of doing. Our biggest challenge was to find local and national sponsors. I got doors slammed in my face, but with enough passion we finally succeeded. That first year 800 women turned out. Then it went from one race to a second race. Now we're in ninety cities, and Race for the Cure is the largest series of 5K fitness runs in the world. This year, more than 700,000 people will participate.

The event works so well because we leave 75 percent of the funds in each community to fund local screening and awareness-education projects. We work together to find the best use for those dollars. The other 25 percent comes back to our national headquarters and is given out in research grants. Our philosophy has always been to support the best research we can find. We typically fund established scientists and postdoctoral candidates who are doing breast-cancer research in their laboratories and clinics. We give away what we raise because we believe it's going to take every bit of it. We are not interested in building the largest endowed foundation in America. We are interested in preventing and curing breast cancer. I want to do that any way I can.

We are now the nation's largest grassroots organization dedicated to fighting breast cancer. We have a staff of about seventy-five people headed by an incredible chief executive officer, Susan Braun. We also have between 30,000 and 40,000 dedicated volunteers throughout the nation working for our cause. In addition to Race for the Cure, we hold a variety of events to raise awareness and provide funds for every kind of problem breast cancer might affect. We are the only organization that addresses the entire spectrum of issues from lab research to the end of life. We know that unless we translate treatment developed in the laboratory to the farthest reaches of the population, we won't make any headway in survival rates. Over the years we've been blessed with tremendous resources to fight this terrible disease. In 1998, foundation revenues were in excess of $50 million. Since our inception, we have raised over $136 million.

> Your mission must become a mantra that you chant over and over and over until people truly grasp it. And you need to be able to articulate it in six seconds or less, because that's the average attention span today.

The most important thing I've learned about building a nonprofit organization is focus, focus, focus, and more focus. You have to be very clear about what you want to do. Your mission must become a mantra that you chant over and over and over until people truly grasp it. And you need to be able to articulate it in six seconds or less, because that's the average attention span today. Then each time you achieve an objective, you have to tell people you've done it. It's really nothing more than brand marketing. Nonprofit organizations have the same challenge any for-profit company does. People need to know that your cause is important and your organization is effective.

were. When I started college at Georgetown, I realized those friend-ships just weren't available for people with mental retardation. I saw a tremendous need for people with disabilities to have opportuni-ties for jobs, public transportation, love, marriage, kids—all those things they weren't getting. I thought that somehow, someway, col-lege kids could help make those opportunities a reality.

At the end of my junior year, I started thinking, "Why can't we bring that model of friendship to this population?" Even though I felt there was a need, I wanted to verify it, so I started visiting with people who ran institutions for those with mental retardation. It quickly became apparent there was a tremendous need, and that college kids could be a great volunteer base. I felt confident I could motivate my fellow students to give their time and energy to this population. So the summer after my junior year, I mapped out a game plan to recruit students in the fall to participate in an organi-zation I would call Best Buddies.

When school started that fall, I put flyers up, got an article in the Georgetown newspaper, and held a recruitment meeting—fifty-two college students came. After that, we paired everyone up with students from the Lt. Joseph P. Kennedy Institute in Washington, D.C., and I started organizing group activities and encouraging the volunteers to meet with their buddies one-on-one. I met with the person from the Institute weekly. I also met with the administration at Georgetown weekly. We became recognized by the university as a campus group, which entitled us to funding to rent buses for group activities. I called a lot of local P.R. representatives in Washington and got free tickets to events so buddies could go to a Washington Bullets game, a Capitols game or a Redskins game. I'd call the stu-dents at night to make sure they were seeing their buddies.

Initially, I had no plans of expanding Best Buddies to other campuses—it just happened. In the fall of '88, a student at Catholic University who had heard about Best Buddies asked me to teach her how to start a chapter. Then I got similar calls from other universities. The late '80s was a perfect time to expand Best Buddies because students had a real desire to get involved and counter the existing stereotype that they were self-absorbed. A lot of colleges, as well, were trying to get students involved in volunteer service. Some campuses even hired a person for the first time to coordinate public-service activities for students.

So the January after I graduated, I decided to spend a year trying to expand Best Buddies. In order to raise funds and give schools a little seed money to run their programs, I decided to hold a ball in Washington, D.C. The ball raised about $60,000, some of which I used as seed money, and some I used to travel around the country speaking to students. I had a good deal of success in California, then pretty much went anywhere I could get an audience. Sometimes I'd stay in the dorms, and sometimes the university would put me up in a campus hotel for free. In those early years, I had a packet of materials I would copy each time I got onto a campus. I'd give speeches and pass out the materials, and programs kind of started on their own.

The following year, I started to formalize the program. Even though I was telling students the same stuff, a lot of them were doing different things on their campuses. So in 1990 I put together a big training conference at Pepperdine University out in L.A. I brought in 150 students and trained them on how to run Best Buddies. It was a very successful conference.

After formalizing the training, I just kept going forward. I started seeking corporate support for Best Buddies, hired a few more people, and created a manual on how to run the thing. I always believed we would have more success if local people ran the program. They understand the local issues: the social climate, the history of their area, the school year, and the type of students. So as quickly as my time and money would allow, I opened offices and hired local staffs. I opened the first office in L.A. to coordinate the success we had in California, then opened a second office in

Chicago. I kept moving around that way depending on where we were most successful.

In the beginning, competition to raise money was huge. I decided early on that people are very curious about how the wealthy live. I thought if we staged events at well-known people's homes, more folks would show up and get turned on to Best Buddies. So I held all of our special events, dinners, and cocktail parties in private homes—never in a hotel, never in a ballroom. I also hoped the people who donated the use of their homes would feel ownership and financial responsibility for Best Buddies and stay with us for a long time. That turned out to be the case.

Most of our growth was from private donations rather than grants. But since money was always an issue, I kept thinking of other ways to raise funds. One way was through Best Buddies Fine Art. It all started when I asked a favorite artist of mine, Keith Haring, to create a logo for us. It turned out to be such a great image that we created a limited-edition silkscreen of 200 and sold them in art galleries. Because that was so successful, and because the art world was on fire in the late '80s, I contacted other artists who had solid mass-market appeal. I asked them if they would create an image depicting what friendship meant to them, let me publish it, and allow the proceeds to go to Best Buddies. Having Keith on board was such a big coup that a lot of other people responded: Roy Lichtenstein, Jim Dine, Romero Britto, and Julian Schnabel. Those images eventually became a series called *The Images of Friendship*. We raised several million dollars from that program alone. The art was so successful that we replicated the concept with a Best Buddies designer T-shirt collection. Gianni Versace, Donna Karan, Giorgio Armani, and others created images we put on apparel.

As celebrities agreed to help us we found that, number one, they became supporters of our organization, and number two, they became role models for Best Buddies. The college students were motivated by the fact that people like Haring and Versace and Karan were all involved. To attract young people, I knew we had to make the organization look "hip" and "happening." I didn't want it to be something that only the nerds on campus did. I wanted the football team and the best-looking guys and girls to get involved too. So that was the concept behind all the unique things we did: hosting events in homes, the logo, the art, the T-shirts, and having celebrities involved. We really wanted to stand out from other groups on campus and do something no one else was doing. This helped us grow faster, since none of the competition could touch us.

Looking back, Best Buddies has really come a long way. That first program in '89 at Georgetown wouldn't meet our standards today. I was shooting from the hip then, trying to come up with activities to keep the program ticking along. Getting fifty-two people involved was a real success. Today, we have nearly 500 chapters, 325 at colleges and about 170 at high schools. We started the high-school program five years after the college program, and it's grown rapidly. We train the students at a leadership conference in Miami for four days every year. We also have staff members visit the campuses throughout the year and make sure the programs are running properly. So there's a much bigger support system today than ever before. During the 1998–99 academic year, 15,000 people volunteered their time and resources for both programs. Since that first chapter, we've had about 85,000 people become Best Buddies.

We still raise a tremendous amount of money to support our operation. Each year events bring us about $1.5 million, and the art program brings us nearly $500,000. The T-shirt program principally operates on college campuses. It's a built-in fund-raising vehicle for the students; they buy the shirts at wholesale and market them at retail. This is a great source of motivation and a way for the students to rally around each other. Although we do things like that to help our local offices raise funds, the national office still supplies a vast majority of their operating income.

I certainly had no idea I'd be doing something like this today.

My first ambition was simply to bring these two diverse populations together, which never would have happened without Best Buddies. As a result, a lot of other things have developed from that simple idea. The students are now teaching people with mental retardation how to get jobs, live independently, do laundry, ride public transportation, get a loan, get married, have kids—things they never thought they could do before. It also helps college and high-school students feel they are contributing in a meaningful way to someone else's life, which builds their self-esteem and improves the quality of their lives. Most important, it teaches them to look for similarities between people rather than differences. And the core of all this is friendship. That's why Best Buddies works.

Our program is very inspiring to me. Day in and day out I see people with disabilities make tremendous progress. One of my first buddies was a guy who lived with his parents. Today, he's completely independent: he's married, lives in his own home, and has a daughter. I'm that kid's godfather! Ten years ago, I never dreamed something like that was a possibility.

I think of another buddy here in Florida who had never held a job. He's now approaching his fourth anniversary as an employee at the Hyatt Hotel. He's also in our Ambassadors Program and flies across the country with me giving speeches about Best Buddies. He talks about what it's like to have a job, be a buddy, have a girlfriend, and all those things. Every time I hear him speak, I know I'm doing the right thing. The change has just been incredible! If I drop dead tomorrow and Best Buddies goes away, that guy's life has been affected forever, and no one can take that away from me or from him, no matter what happens.

These two buddies are very close to me, but there are others all over the country having similar experiences. Parents write to me and say their son or daughter had never been anywhere without them until Best Buddies came along. No one had ever called them on the telephone, no one had ever offered friendship, no one had

ever helped them find a job. So Best Buddies provides a huge relief
and support system for families. Just as important, when a kid from
Harvard or Yale or Stanford befriends a buddy, it reassures the parents that their son or daughter with mental retardation does have
value. This brings great joy to fathers and mothers all over the
world.

I think it takes several things to make a nonprofit organization
work. First, you've got to live and breathe your cause on a daily basis
for the first five to ten years. You've got to have so much passion that
you won't take no for an answer. If you don't have
this kind of passion, you should wrap it up,
because there are so many obstacles. Getting a
nonprofit going and keeping it going is incredibly
time-consuming. Some days I think I'm wed to
Best Buddies for life. [Laughs.]

Second, you've got to have a tremendous
work ethic. You've got to be willing to work like a
dog to get your issue across and sell people on it.
I think people saw that this cause was my life, and

> Everyone wants to
> invest in a winner. If
> people question
> your work ethic and
> commitment, you're
> in for a very, very
> rocky road.

that I would work hard enough to make it succeed. They knew if
they gave me 10 grand, I was going to make it 50; and if they gave
me 50 grand, I was going to make it 150. Everyone wants to invest
in a winner. If people question your work ethic and commitment,
you're in for a very, very rocky road.

Third, you've got to figure out ways to generate revenue to support your effort. It's a very large mistake to get people involved and
start touching lives, then falter because you don't have enough
resources to support your work. With Best Buddies, people with
mental retardation have became accustomed to having friendship
and seeing their lives change and become more fulfilling. If the program disappears because there is no money to support it, people's
lives could be devastated.

Anyway, this work has brought tremendous joy into my life.

There are more benefits than I ever dreamed possible, both personally and professionally. I learned this from my parents growing up:
the more you give, the more you get. Sometimes you say that to
young people, and they're like, "Yeah, yeah, yeah," but it really is
true. I met my wife through Best Buddies, and she's the most important thing in the world to me. My kids are also involved, and so are
80 percent of my friends. Doing service is a great way to get to know
people and bring our communities together. If all the lonely people
in America would just volunteer in a service organization, their
loneliness would go out the door; they'd get to know more people
than they ever imagined. I have friends in cities all over America,
not because I'm such a great guy, but because they're all involved in
Best Buddies. Buddies brought us all together, and that's made my
life very, very rewarding.

MIMI SILBERT

*Mimi Silbert is the founder of Delancey Street, a residential edu-
cation center for ex-convicts and substance abusers. This extraordinary organization, headquartered in San Francisco, has
facilities throughout the country where residents receive a high-
school education and are trained in three different marketable
skills. More than 12,000 men and women have graduated from
Delancey Street and are now leading successful lives as lawyers,
truck drivers, medical professionals, and even law-enforcement
officers. Here's Mimi's story:*

I was teaching criminology and psychology at U.C. Berkeley. I was
also working as a prison psychologist and a group therapist in private practice. It didn't take me long to realize that everything we
were doing with the prison population was wrong. It didn't matter
how much brilliant therapy I provided; focusing on people's internal problems was not the long-term solution. Most of the people
who fill up our prisons come from the underclass and are genera-

tionally poor. They don't know the first thing about making it in the mainstream—they don't know it attitudinally and they don't know it behaviorally. It's like they are from a foreign country and need to learn a whole new culture for living successfully.

My own upbringing provided real insights for the new model we created. I grew up in an immigrant ghetto in Boston. My grandparents, parents, aunts, and uncles all lived together in very close quarters. We all supported each other and worked hard to achieve the American dream. Eventually, we all moved up and purchased our own homes, but we remained very close. My Mom's brothers lived next door to each other, and my Mom and Dad were right around the corner from them. So the extended family concept helped us succeed—we all worked to better ourselves and our family. In fact, I became an overachiever; I earned two master's degrees and two Ph.D.s, and I even had twins instead of one kid. [Laughs.]

Somehow, the people I was working with in the prison system missed out on this experience. The idea that everyone has a shot at the American dream was totally foreign to them. I think the real horror of our ghettos today is that people become generationally trapped there. Consequently, they end up becoming passive recipients of all kinds of things: the left gives them excuses and therapy, and the right gives them punishments. Neither political party ever stops to say, "We need these people in our country, so let's teach them to become active doers."

About this same time, I started a clinic in the U.C. Berkeley Law School with a brilliant psychiatrist named Bernard Diamond and a great professor named Richard Korn. We were experimenting with the concept of giving as a way of getting healthy. The idea came to me as I was doing therapy. Everyone I worked with was forever saying, "Thank you, thank you, thank you, Mimi, for helping me!" It made me think, "What a good girl you are, Mimi, for helping all these people." Until one day it struck me: Who would want to be the person having to say thanks all the time? So we were testing the idea that helping others is the best way to help yourself. It gives you a sense of who you are and what you have to offer. The concept was, when A helps B, A will get better. B may or may not improve, but if B helps C, B will get better too.

Anyway, our work was written up in the news, and a visionary man named John Maher contacted me. John was an ex-convict who had started a place for ex-felons. Originally, he asked me to help him write a grant to get some federal money. As we talked about it, we agreed that was a horrible idea. We realized we thought exactly alike on how to best help people. So in 1971 I joined him to develop the Delancey Street model, with the purpose of helping ex-convicts become part of a healthy community. The organization was designed around the extended family concept, where all residents need to be productive, not just to better themselves but also to help the family grow for the next generation. It's named after a street on the lower east side of New York where immigrants lived in extended families, supported one another, and together made their way into America. So I put aside all of the brilliant theories I was teaching and went back to the basics.

A few people in our original group were earning money, so we pooled our resources. Then we did what fifteen friends would do if they decided to form their own extended family. We asked, "Who can cook?" and that person became the head of our food services department. Next we asked, "Who has ever hammered a nail?" and that person became the head of construction. Our goal was to have each member become an active contributor rather than a passive recipient and eventually earn money as a group so we could survive. We were just like an immigrant family where Daddy put his money in if he made it, Mommy put her money in if she made it, and the children put their money in if they made it.

Initially, we rented places to live in. Then in 1972, we bought the former Russian Consulate in Pacific Heights, the most exclusive section of San Francisco. It had been vacated and was run down, but it was in a magnificent neighborhood. Because it had never been rezoned and turned into apartments, it was cheaper than buying an apartment building. It really was a perfect neighborhood for us, because we wanted our people to become everything these neighbors were. Unfortunately, the neighborhood went completely crazy when we bought the house; everyone thought crime would go up and property values would go down. We decided to show them we would be the best neighbors possible, even though we were ex-cons and ex-drug addicts. John used the line, "You can't cure an alcoholic in a bar." So we taught our people construction skills and renovated the building—we really did an excellent job! We also did crime patrols before neighborhood watches existed. Consequently, crime went down.

Another thing we did to make friends was volunteer our services. We told people, "We have able bodies and will help in any way we can." One day some neighbors asked us to clear out their home because they were having a benefit for the Ballet. As the boss, I was standing there dutifully when one of the guys picked up a piano and said, "Uh, Mimi, whatta ya want me ta do with this?" I looked over at him, and a light bulb went off inside my head. I said to myself, "That's it! These guys have been pumping iron in prison for years so they could come to Delancey Street and start a moving company!" Meanwhile, the guy was still standing there with this piano going, "Uh, do you want me to put it inside or outside?"

That very day, we came home and made flyers that said "MOVING? WE WILL DO IT FOR LESS!" We put them under every windshield wiper we could find. We did this over and over until someone actually called us. When this person finished describing the job, we said, "I'll call you right back." We called another moving company, explained the job, got their quote, then called the customer back and offered to do it for less. [Laughs.] We rented little green uniforms and a Hertz truck and all marched off to this moving job. Since we make our guys cut their hair short, we were very middle-class looking. We did the job in about one second because we had some serious arms in the group! [Laughs.]

The people were thrilled and recommended us for more jobs. After a while we were renting a truck regularly; then we bought our own truck. One day someone from the government knocked on our door and said, "What do you think you're doing?" It turns out that moving is a licensed and regulated industry. Our answer became our motto at Delancey Street: "Oh, I'm sorry, we didn't know. Please teach us what we need to do, and we'll fix the mistake." [Laughs.] That little moving venture is now a national company—Delancey Street Movers. In San Francisco alone, we have forty-five trucks and a number of diesel rigs. Almost everyone in our program learns to drive a diesel rig as one of their marketable skills. They graduate and make more money then I ever did as a college professor! This became the first of many businesses we have started to support our organization and serve as training schools for our residents.

Here's how Delancey Street works today. The people who come here—either on their own or through the judicial system—are drug addicts, ex-cons, and homeless people. We take anyone who has hit bottom for any reason, except for sexual offenders who need professional counseling we don't provide. Some are facing life in prison; others have overdosed a number of times and might die next time. A lot of other programs would never take these people, so we are a court of last resort. The first thing we do is explain our three rules: no drugs or alcohol, no physical violence, and no threats of violence. I tell them, "I don't know why you do these things. Maybe it's environmental. Maybe you are missing a chromosome. I don't care. You just can't do them ever again. So that's solved." The real issue is to learn to be successful and productive without drugs and crime. Anyone who is willing to accept our very structured environment is welcome. If they break the three primary rules, they're kicked out of the program. All other mistakes we teach them to fix.

Each new resident is then placed in what we call a minion of ten people. The minion leader, who has been there a little longer, tells them they are not only responsible for themselves but for each other as well. One of the difficult things we have to do is break the code of silence that exists on the street, where no one tells anything about anyone. We help them understand that if a group member starts doing something that is self-destructive, they need to take action; if they don't, that person might die. Eventually these ten people become a true unit.

The first thing we teach our residents are personal skills: how to face themselves, how to break old habits, how to deal with change, how to get along with other people, and how to learn to love. Since many of them have been homeless, we also teach basic personal hygiene: how to take a shower, how to dress, how to clean your clothes. In addition, most of these people have never had jobs before, so we teach them basic work habits like showing up on time, listening to a boss, and getting along with coworkers. As soon as they show they are responsible and can get along with others without growling and grumbling, they enter one of our vocational training schools.

Our residents learn at least three marketable skills while they are at Delancey Street. In these rapidly changing times, we want them to be able to shift into different careers as necessary. Along with our moving company, we have a number of money-making ventures that serve as training grounds for our people. One of our more successful schools is our construction program. We started off doing renovations and eventually built our own complex. Many of our graduates have become general contractors, electrical contractors, and plumbing contractors. We also have a printing company that makes banners, buttons, and other advertising materials. We have Christmas tree lots where we not only sell trees, but we also decorate large buildings during the holidays. We have a huge restaurant that has been well reviewed—the Delancey Street Restaurant. In New Mexico, we have an incredible hand-hewn furniture-making operation that sells Taos-style furniture to individuals, hotels, and government offices. And we've recently opened the Crossroads Café, which is a café, juice bar, bookstore, and art gallery.

These businesses are run as training schools within the Delancey Street Foundation. Our residents teach the courses and run the programs—we have no professional staff. Our people start at the bottom, then work their way up as they demonstrate responsibility. For example, they can move from automotive repair to truck repair to our diesel rigs. In our sales department, they can learn basic sales techniques, then move all the way up to advertising specialty sales. In the restaurant, they can go from dishwasher to prep cook to line cook to managing chef. It's tremendous on-the-job training!

Each of these training-schools/businesses has been started with that entrepreneurial spirit. We always say, "Okay, we need money to stay alive, and there's an opportunity here. We just need to learn how to do this, then do it better than anyone else." So we jump in, work hard, and usually come out winners! The best example of this is the multimillion dollar complex we built by ourselves. No one thought we could do it! People patted me on the head and said, "You're wonderful at what you do, but we're talking about serious construction now." But we did it! I was the developer, and we were our own general contractor. We sold off one of the buildings we owned and acquired a piece of property on the south waterfront, which had not been developed yet. We started building with our own money while banks continued turning us down for loans. What I wanted was a $4 million unrestricted loan so we could say, "We are building *our* new home." I didn't want our 350 former drug addicts who had never worked before getting up each day and saying, "Here we go again to build Blipity Bank's building."

Finally, Bank of America gave us the loan when no one else would. What happened was, our printing company did some work for Tom Clauson, the CEO of Bank of America at the time. We made him 10,000 "No Takeover" buttons to protest a pending acquisition by another bank. The buttons were a big hit, so they ordered 50,000. We said, "No problem!" I woke everybody up, and we worked all night to produce the buttons. Then they called back and said they needed 100,000 more. Again, we said, "No problem!" We had to stop everything we were doing to make these buttons. In a press conference to announce our loan, Tom Clauson got up and told that story. Then he said, "So when Mimi called me and said she wanted a $4 million unsecured loan for a building to be built by her as the developer (never having developed anything before) and 350 ex-convicts (who had never worked before and didn't know the construction trade) and that she would pay us back from their seasonal Christmas tree sales, I told her, 'No problem!'" [Laughs.] And that is precisely what we did! We built a beautiful 400,000-square-foot complex and paid back the four-year loan in three years, primarily with our own revenues.

We now have 500 residents in San Francisco, 500 in Los Angeles, and nearly 1,000 in facilities in New York, New Mexico, and North Carolina. Residents work though our programs the same way they would if they were going to college. And like college students, they stay an average of four years. Along with the vocational skills, they can take courses in Russian, world literature, geometry, and many other subjects that help them become well-rounded individuals. I always tell people we are the Harvard of the underclass. Just like Harvard takes the top 2 percent, we take the bottom 2 percent. [Laughs.] But our people leave with the academics, three marketable career skills, and lots of survival and interpersonal skills. So I think we are better than Harvard. I know we have a better football team. [Laughs.]

The best thing about Delancey Street is seeing our residents change. The majority of them have been through other programs, and they think everything is a hustle. When they come here they keep saying, "Losers like us don't live in gorgeous buildings like this.

Where is the con?" They keep thinking somebody up there is selling dope and they'll get in on it soon. That's fine with me because their curiosity gets them through the adjustment period. Eventually they figure out it's real and make amazing changes in their lives. They not only get skilled at being legitimate and successful, they also gain decency and integrity. They get rid of their prejudices, they care about making society better, and they help children and seniors in need. Every story is so moving you almost believe it's too good to be true. I love the courage our residents display and who they become!

Someone once did a ten-year study that showed our success rate is over 90 percent, but I don't like statistics like that. We've been around for twenty-eight years and have more than 12,000 successful graduates. How is anyone going to keep track of what these people do from day to day? What I am comfortable saying is that we are the exact opposite of the prison system, which costs taxpayers $40,000 a year to keep each prisoner alive—not to mention the hundreds of millions spent building facilities. Delancey Street costs taxpayers nothing! It is supported by our own revenue, and the residents serve as our staff. Most of our graduates—who were once at the bottom of society—are now thriving, taxpaying citizens. It's just incredible what people can do when you give them structure, support, and lots of love. It worked in my family, and it works here.

Finally, I think volunteering is the best thing in the whole world. I've done this for twenty-eight years without a salary, so I guess I am the quintessential volunteer of an all-volunteer organization. I can tell you there is absolutely nothing in life as exciting as giving of yourself and seeing lives change. As a volunteer, you might be that person who walks in the door and ends up changing a life!

> We are the exact opposite of the prison system, which costs taxpayers $40,000 a year to keep each prisoner alive. Delancey Street costs taxpayers nothing! It is supported by our own revenue.

PATIENCE WHITE

Patience White is the founder of the Adolescent Employment Readiness Center (AERC), located in the Children's National Medical Center in Washington, D.C. The AERC provides a number of services to improve the employability of adolescents, twelve to twenty-one years of age, with chronic illnesses and physical disabilities. To date, the AERC has helped 1,500 young people with cerebral palsy, diabetes, cancer, spina bifida, cystic fibrosis, and many other illnesses prepare for competitive employment in the workforce.

Two things led me to where I am today. First, I got a degree in socioeconomics from Vassar, then went to Venezuela and worked in the slums of Caracas. I was interested in the infrastructure for economic development in the country. At the time, Venezuela was moving from an agrarian to an industrial society, and thousands of people were leaving the jungles and looking for food and work. A lot of these people were ill and had the opportunity to work in a local clinic. It was an incredible experience that left a real impression on me. Instead of coming back and applying for a Ph.D. in economics, I decided to go to medical school—the second thing that led me to where I am today.

I got my medical degree at Harvard and did my training in internal medicine. During this time, I was studying people with arthritis because I thought it was going to be a major health issue. I ran into my pediatrician, Dr. Sydney Stillman, whom I consider the father of pediatric rheumatology in the United States. He told me about his work, and I became very interested in children with disabilities. Eventually I went to England and studied pediatric rheumatology with Dr. Barbara Ansell. While I was there, I observed how they dealt with disability, which was quite a bit different than what we were doing here. I put that information in the back of my mind and came back to the United States.

When I returned, I got a job in Washington, D.C., practicing both pediatric and adult rheumatology. I found myself asking very different questions while working in the two departments. When I saw young people in the pediatric clinic, I asked them about school, friends, and family. When they transitioned into my adult clinic, I asked about their jobs, social life, and future plans. It became obvious that some young people with arthritis were not functioning very well when they reached adulthood. Most of them were doing very little planning for their future, especially in the area of employment readiness. When I put on my economics hat, I said, "This doesn't make any sense."

I started looking for programs that would meet the needs of my patients. I discovered that vocational rehabilitation in the federal system didn't start until the kids were eighteen. Also, the special-education programs in the schools focused primarily on kids with cognitive disabilities like mental retardation. It became obvious that existing programs either didn't meet the needs or started way too late. I decided something needed to be done to help young people with physical disabilities prepare for competitive employment. After ten years of practice, I knew how to manage their medical illnesses with the right medication, but if they sat home and never participated in adult society, it hurt everybody. So I figured this was more important than the drugs I could give. I had the passion and determination, and I figured it would be easy. [Laughs.]

The first thing I did was apply for a grant to study the career maturity of young people with chronic illnesses. I received a three-year research grant from the Maternal and Child Health Bureau. The study revealed some interesting findings. First, we learned that teenagers with serious illnesses were just as interested in careers as their healthy counterparts, which was very good news. Second, we found that kids with disabilities knew a lot less about the requirements of jobs than their healthy peers, which was not good news. And third, we discovered that parents thought their nondisabled children should have a first work experience at the age of thirteen—

such as paper routes and babysitting—but parents of children with disabilities felt their kids should have a first job experience at sixteen, which put them three years behind their peers. So the study showed that teenagers with physical illnesses are interested in jobs but may fall behind because of limited workplace knowledge and perceptions about their abilities. I was thrilled with these findings because I felt we could make a difference. It was fantastic!

I started visiting big employers in the area to enlist their support. As brash as I was, I would call up the president and say, "I want to come talk to your board." Early on, some extraordinary people let me talk to them. I pitched the program in two ways to catch their attention. First, I explained the enormous need: approximately 20 percent of all teens in this country have some type of chronic illness or disability, and because our medical system is so good, most of them survive and live long lives. Unfortunately, many of these kids become adults who don't work and who receive welfare. So I suggested to these companies that this was a good opportunity to help these young people. Second, I showed them how much money we could save society for each youth with a disability we transitioned off welfare. I took a financial sheet with me that showed the cost of multiplying monthly welfare payments times twenty to thirty years. It was pretty easy to see the financial implications of getting youth with disabilities off welfare and into the workforce. Consequently, a number of these employers agreed to help me design the program, provide internships for the kids, and assist with fund-raising.

> Approximately 20 percent of all teens in this country have some type of chronic illness or disability. Unfortunately, many of these kids become adults who don't work and who receive welfare.

From the beginning, I knew we had to reach kids at eleven or twelve years of age and include the entire family in the program. If we didn't, we would never change expectations about the work capacity of children with disabilities. I also knew we had to assist them through high school and on to higher education. The data is pretty clear: the more education you get, the more money you make; the more money you make, the more capable you are of buying health insurance. In addition, I felt the program needed to be placed in a health-care system as opposed to a federal facility or vocational rehabilitation center. At the time, the majority of kids with chronic illnesses in the surrounding tri-state area were coming to the Children's National Medical Center here in Washington, D.C. So we created a career program right inside the hospital, then notified all the clinics that our employment readiness services were available. Before long, people began referring kids to us.

What we have today is a career center to support adolescents, twelve to twenty-one years of age, with a variety of chronic illnesses and disabilities. Our goal is to prepare them for competitive employment in the workforce, just like anybody else. We serve kids with diabetes, cancer, paraplegia, cystic fibrosis, rheumatic diseases, cerebral palsy, asthma, spina bifida—you name it, we deal with it. Initially, we start by meeting with their parents. We talk to them about expectations, possibilities, and how to best help their child succeed. Interestingly enough, studies show that disabled people say that being asked to do chores when they were young was important to their success. I must admit, my children don't agree. [Laughs.] So we encourage parents to give their kids chores and help them have a work experience by the age of thirteen. Many of these parents get involved in our Parent Advisory Council.

One of the first things we do with the kids is give them interest tests to find out what kind of career work they might enjoy. Then we do a number of things to help them learn about various careers and organizations. We offer job readiness sessions, educational events, work experiences with companies, and internships. One of our more successful programs is our Career Awareness Day. This is a one-day conference that brings together business, education, parents, regional service organizations, and adolescents with disabilities. The conference is designed to give these young people both information and skills. They participate in workshops with employers and actually go through mock job interviews. The employers come back every year because they learn about the full spectrum of disabilities and what this means to their future workforce. More than 200 employers have participated in this conference.

Over the years we've seen wonderful changes in the young people we work with. Here are a few examples: Lorenzo Stewart was shot twice in the back when he was fifteen years old by a person he never saw—it left him paralyzed from the waist down. He entered our program after spending four months in the hospital. At first he was angry and very depressed. It took us over a year to get him interested in his future, but he finally landed a job with an investment group. I think that was the first time he felt like he had a real future. He went on to finish high school and is now going to college. He is working part-time and helping other disabled students just like himself. Then there is Ebony. She is a young lady with severe diabetes. She had been in and out of school and was not functioning very well. She entered our program at a real low point. She has now finished college, is fully employed, and is thinking about going to law school. It is so rewarding to see these young people enter our program, often down and out, then become very productive adults. They all turn out to be wonderful people.

Since we began in the mid '80s, we've had about 1,500 kids go through the program. We have a small staff that includes a program coordinator, a vocational counselor, a job developer, and an outreach coordinator. We work with anywhere from thirty to sixty young people each month. Early on, we were funded mostly by federal grants; we now receive contributions from foundations and businesses as well. I think it's critical that businesses support us; if they don't, there is no point in having the program.

People now come here from all over the world to look at what we are doing. I've also been to England, Sweden, Australia, Israel, and

Finland to talk about our program. I think we've been successful because we don't duplicate anybody else's services. This was critical to gaining support in the beginning. We have also gotten the right stakeholders together. When you have the right people around the table, solutions become obvious. It's amazing how well we can solve our own problems; we don't always need the government to do it for us.

I compare this work to planting a big garden. You spread these little seeds around and they all grow up. Each one will be a little bit different, but that's fantastic! And every teenager we get off the streets and into the workplace is much better off. The amazing thing is that once they make it, they often help others, just as Lorenzo is doing. So if you get two kids involved, they help two more, and they help two more, and so on. What we are doing is trying to reclaim the streets of D.C. one kid at a time. [Laughs.]

CHAPTER · 5

FEEDING OUR HUNGRY

There are people in the world so hungry, that God cannot appear to them except in the form of bread.

MAHATMA GANDHI

If you can't feed a hundred people, then feed just one.

MOTHER TERESA

It seems to me that our three basic needs, for food and security and love, are so mixed and mingled and entwined that we cannot straightly think of one without the others.

M.F.K. FISHER

As Rita Ungaro-Schiavone entered the small, one-room apartment, she met Mr. And Mrs. Smith. Handicapped and paraplegic, Mr. Smith sat in his wheelchair dressed in only a T-shirt, his thin legs draped with a towel. Mrs. Smith was a frail little lady who suffered constant pain from cancer and other serious ailments. Although they were very poor, disabled, and often hungry, this elderly couple struggled to maintain their independence. In spite of their efforts, the floor was dirty, the bed linens were discolored, and the general condition of their apartment would be considered unlivable by many.

When Rita asked them if they had considered a nursing home, Mr. Smith firmly explained, "My wife and I were both employed in nursing homes all of our lives. We don't want to go there. We want our independence. I get up in the morning when I want to get up. I eat when I want to. I watch television when I want to watch it, and I watch the shows I choose. I go to bed when I want to. In a nursing home, we will no longer make such decisions about our lives. We will be told what to do and when to do it. It isn't much, but this is *our* home."

Rita, the founder of Aid For Friends, arranged to have a group of volunteers from Temple University clean the apartment from top to bottom and provide new bed linens. Next, she arranged for a volunteer to visit the Smiths each week and deliver seven nutritious meals cooked by members of St. Jerome's Parish. In addition to the food, this volunteer befriended the couple and helped meet their basics needs. With this new support system, the Smiths were able to get the nutrition they desperately needed, maintain the independence they treasured, and live relatively comfortable lives.

Unfortunately, many of the homebound have serious problems. A study by the Urban Institute shows that 2.5 million elderly are not sure where their next meal will come from. Every month they have to choose between buying groceries or paying their bills. Being financially and physically unable to buy food and prepare nutritious meals, they suffer from hunger, malnutrition, and hunger-related diseases.

According to the USDA, more than eleven million people in America are going hungry each day, and twenty-five million more are considered food insecure—they regularly skip meals or reduce the size of their meals. Many of these people—who are unemployed, underemployed, or physically and mentally disadvantaged—go days without eating a nutritious meal. As mentioned earlier, fourteen million of the thirty-six million hungry in this country are children—approximately 40 percent. These kids begin their day hungry and go to bed hungry. They also suffer from the physical consequences of hunger: infant mortality, anemia, learning disabilities, and other types of hunger-related illnesses. Hungry children have a difficult time reaching their physical and intellectual potential. Worldwide the problem is much worse. According to the World Bank, one billion people in the world live in poverty, which means they also go hungry. Tragically, 40,000 children die every day of starvation.

Despite this hunger crisis, there is ample food in America to feed our people. A recent study by the USDA shows that ninety-six billion pounds of food are lost every year at the retail and food-service levels. This equates to 25 percent of the 356 billion pounds of food we produce in this country each year. This startling figure promoted the USDA to meet with nonprofit organizations in the first National Summit on Food Recovery in 1997. At this conference, a goal was set to increase by 33 percent the amount of food recovered nationally by the year 2000. This will provide an additional 500 million pounds of food each year for hungry people. To achieve this objective, the USDA is working with the National Restaurant Association to produce a food recovery handbook for its members, and it is encouraging the Department of Transportation to develop methods for transporting recovered food.

In this chapter you will meet five social entrepreneurs who have approached the problem of hunger in unique and effective ways. Rita Ungaro-Schiavone has organized an army of volunteers to prepare extra servings of their regular dinners, then donate them to the elderly in Philadelphia. Bea Gaddy started gathering leftover food from local grocery stores and sharing it with her neighbors; now she feeds the poor in Baltimore. Billy Shore has created an incredible organization that generates wealth to fund grassroots hunger organizations. Paulette Hardin and a group of compassionate souls started SHARE to reduce the cost of monthly groceries; families pay $14 and get $30 worth of food each month provided they volunteer to help with packaging and distribution. And Joseph Grassi has created and promoted an idea that brings thousands of individuals into the fight against hunger; they skip one meal each week and donate the savings to hunger organizations.

RITA UNGARO-SCHIAVONE

Rita Ungaro-Schiavone is the founder of Aid For Friends, an interfaith organization formed to provide free food and friendship to needy shut-ins, primarily the frail elderly. Aid For Friends currently has 12,000 volunteers who cook and deliver 800,000 meals a year to homebound individuals. The idea for providing this service came to Rita when she began making weekly visits to a blind and bedridden elderly woman in Philadelphia. Here's Rita's story:

My involvement in serving the hungry really began when I was asked to collect food for a group that was taking in gang members. Later, I established a community food distribution program for the Archdiocese of Philadelphia. We had twenty-four emergency food centers throughout five counties. Even though it was organized through the Catholic church it served the whole community.

In 1974 I decided to go back to college. I had not finished my degree because I got married and started having babies right away—like most Catholics during the '50s. [Laughs.] I wanted to get a bachelor's/master's combination, then a Ph.D., but it never happened. My plan was to continue doing charitable work while I was in school, so I went to the Frankford YWCA and told the director, Marian Dockhorn, I would give her a half day every week. She gave me a list of eleven shut-ins in the community who had called and asked for help. As I visited them, I found they all had two things in common: they were hungry, and they were lonely.

The first person I visited was a sweet, lovely lady named Minnie. Her house was insufferably hot and dark. She said she didn't mind the darkness because she was blind. She had a daughter who was leaning against the wall, practically catatonic from depression. As

Minnie sat on her bed with her atrophied legs dangling over the edge, I asked if I could get her something cold to drink. I was alarmed to find there was no food in the kitchen. I came back with a glass of water and said, "You know, it's getting close to lunchtime and I'm hungry. How about if I get us some sandwiches?" So I went to a nearby delicatessen and got some lunch, and we ate together. Before I left, I asked her if I could come back tomorrow with a few things; I've learned always to ask for permission to help someone. She said that would be fine.

That night, I cooked a skillet dinner for my family with ground beef, broth, tomatoes, corn, and rice. As we were eating, I said to my husband and four sons, "This would really be good for Minnie and her daughter." So I took heavy-duty foil, wrapped up several servings, and put them in the freezer. The next day I went back with a friend of mine who was a nurse and took a fan, bed linens, and the food. I heated up the frozen dinners and served them to Minnie and her daughter. That was Aid For Friends' first meal—the first of nine million.

I decided that what these shut-ins needed were good, home-cooked meals every day, plus friendship. I went to my fellow parishioners at St. Jerome's Church and told them what I wanted to do. In one of our meetings, somebody suggested we get aluminum TV dinner trays, which we did. The idea was to have families cook an extra portion of their dinner, put it in a tray, and place it in their freezer. Once a week, volunteer drivers would go to the cooks' homes, pick up the frozen dinners, and take them to a central freezer for later distribution. Other volunteers would then take seven meals to an elderly shut-in each week and visit for an hour.

Early on, I was invited to speak to the ministers and priests at the Frankford Ministerium to explain our program. A pastor named Reverend La Vonne Althouse asked me to speak to her congregation at the Salem Lutheran Church, which blew me away. At the time, Roman Catholic women did not stand at the altars, let alone give sermons. After that, I was asked to speak to a group at a Jewish synagogue. Other priests asked me to speak at their churches as well. This started a whole new ministry for me as I tried to motivate people to volunteer and expand our free services. What really brought attention to our program was being on the radio. Through an early volunteer, I was introduced to Bernard Meltzer, the host of a popular Philadelphia radio talk show. Aid For Friends became his favorite charity, and he frequently invited me to be on his show. Listeners started sending in donations. Many of these people still support the program today.

We now work with six synagogues and more than 200 Catholic and Protestant churches on a regular basis. They supply cooks, drivers, and visitors for our homebound friends. Our meals come from three sources. First, we receive home-cooked meals from individuals and families who make extra servings—this is about half of our meals. Second, we have churches, synagogues, schools, and other groups get together and cook 20, 100, or 500 meals at a time. St. Ignatius Church, for example, provided 12,000 meals last year. As part of this effort, we have schoolchildren and youth groups collect nonperishable breakfast items and place them in bags with homemade greeting cards. Third, we provide low-sodium dinners that have been mandated by the doctors of our shut-ins. Volunteers purchase the food with donations we receive and cook these special meals. We now have 260 freezers in five counties for the collection, storage, and distribution of Aid For Friends' meals.

There have been a few times we didn't have enough meals because of power failure. On one of these occasions, I called my pastor, Father Graham, and asked him to make an announcement at the daily masses that we needed people to help. That afternoon he was there with two teenagers asking for 500 trays. He's a gourmet cook, among his other talents. He got the teenagers to help him cook and our retired pastor to pack the trays and cover them with foil. Now I know if I ask him to make an announcement, he's going to be over in the afternoon asking for trays.

We now have nearly 12,000 active volunteers. Some of these people are poor themselves, but they are very generous to others in their neighborhoods. One time we went into a needy area to recruit, and a woman said to me, "Well, I can make you one meal a week. I can't make more than that because sometimes we just have cereal for dinner." I asked her to make one meal a month instead of one a week. It's really a miracle what people are doing. Our visitor volunteers are particularly important to the program. We ask them to give up one hour a week to deliver seven meals and visit with their new homebound friend. This is so important because people experience God's love through the compassion of other human beings. That's how God uses us; we're his hands and heart.

Most of the people we visit are referred to us by hospitals, nursing agencies, or home health agencies. We now serve more than 2,000 disabled elderly shut-ins who can't shop or cook for themselves.

So many individuals come to mind, but one that stands out is Dorothy. It was a freezing winter day when I knocked on the door of her badly neglected house. She came to the door in an old winter coat that was held together by safety pins. When I went in, I noticed it was just as cold inside as it was outside. The place was in shambles! She told me she hadn't had heating oil for two weeks and was out of food. She said she was thinking about taking some rat poison she had found because she couldn't stand it anymore. Well, I made arrangements to get her some heating oil, then took seven meals over to her house. She was so hungry she didn't want to wait for the first one to defrost. As I got to know her,

> Our visitor volunteers are particularly important. We ask them to give up one hour a week to deliver seven meals and visit with their new homebound friend. This is so important because people experience God's love through the compassion of other human beings.

I learned she was a fifty-seven-year-old who had never matured into adulthood. Her parents were dead, and a couple that befriended her had drained her bank account. During the three years I visited her, I got her some new clothes, tried to raise her self-esteem, sold her house, and found her an apartment with a side porch. When she died, I realized how fond I had become of this very special woman. She is one of hundreds I could tell you about.

Anyway, last year was our best year yet. We delivered more than 550,000 dinners, 80,000 containers of home-made soup, and 20,000 breakfast bags. Most of our food is donated. Last year we received nearly $2.5 million of in-kind donations. We also receive financial support from 3,000 donors. If you account for the food, people's time, and donations, we provide about $6 million in annual services. When the government provides meals to the elderly, it costs $5 a meal, and that doesn't include delivery. It's difficult to compare the cost of our meals, because we do so many other things. We provide friendship, nutritional supplements, emergency financial assistance, and safety items like tub grab bars and bathtub seats. We also give gifts like jogging suits, sweaters, night wear, bed slippers, and handmade afghans. We focus on gifts of warmth because elderly people often have poor circulation and get cold easily.

To keep the organization going, we still do a lot of speaking to recruit volunteers. I did all of it myself when I was younger. Now I have others who go out to churches, synagogues, and schools. In addition, we send out a newsletter that tells our story to thousands of readers. It contains a story about one of our shut-ins and information about nutrition, food safety, and fund-raisers we might be having. It also contains instructions for becoming a volunteer or financial supporter.

If I had known in the early years we would grow to the size we are now, I would have been terrified. I dreamed big dreams to help others because I knew the Lord would be with me, but I had no idea we would serve more than nine million meals to shut-ins over the years. It's funny how things work out. I traded my dream of going back to school for a new dream: to serve as many of the homebound as possible. These are forgotten people nobody cares about, including some of their families. But we can be their friends. My motto is, "Food and friendship: little miracles love can bring." One of our shut-ins recently wrote, "Thank you for coming into my life. You have respected me and cared about me. The reason your program has become so important to me is explained in your name, Aid For Friends. That's what I have received from you—your friendship."

All of this came about with help from key advisers, wonderful, volunteers and an unbelievable staff. For our board, I've always looked for people with expertise in social work or public health, for clergy not bankers. Most nonprofit organizations do it the other way around, but I really believe in providence. If we pray and ask for God's help, he sends us help when we need it—and he sent us these wonderful people. Actually, I believe we're all called to be good Samaritans, regardless of our religion or economic level. And we should give without expectation of reward; if we receive gratitude, it's just icing on the cake. But we must not try and change people; just love them, respond to their needs, and be a friend. Then wonderful things happen.

BEA GADDY

Bea Gaddy is the founder of the Bea Gaddy Family Centers, Inc., a network of centers dedicated to feeding needy people and also teaching them about self-worth and self-reliance. Her idea developed as she wheeled a garbage can around to small grocery stores collecting food for her hungry children and neighbors. She now serves Thanksgiving dinner to 45,000 people and provides additional services to more than 80,000. Here's Bea's story:

I had five children and worked at a hospital here in Baltimore. After four years I had to quit because I couldn't find anybody to keep the children. I worked at various jobs but basically became a welfare mother. I had food stamps, medical assistance, and all that. Life went on, but it wasn't a happy time. I had not learned what self-worth meant and was very low in spirits. When I finally sank to the bottom I started praying to God. I asked him to show me how to feed myself and my children consistently instead of piecemeal, with two weeks of eating well and then no food. What came to my mind was to do an emergency food center.

I went to my pastor and asked him if I could use one of his large garbage cans that had wheels on it. There were three little grocery stores in our neighborhood, and I went to the first one with this garbage can. I asked the man at the store if he would give me the food he was going to throw away that night. He gave me a funny look and said, "All right," then started putting food into this garbage can. I took the food back to our two-bedroom apartment on Patterson Park Avenue. As I walked past the houses on my street, I could see the window shades and curtains moving—people were laughing at me.

I then went to the second store, which was directly across the street, and said to the man there, "Sir, would you please give me the food you are going to throw away tonight so we can eat?" Hesitating, he asked, "What did you say?" He just knew I was crazy. But after a moment he started putting food into the garbage can and almost filled it. I took that food back across the street, and my neighbors were still peepin' out their windows. No one came out and said, "Bea, I'll help you," so I just put all the food in the hallway.

I went to the third store with my garbage can, and this man said, "Bea, what are you doing?" I told him I was trying to collect food so we could eat—myself, my children, and other people on the block. I really hadn't planned on feeding anybody else at first, not the people next door and especially not thousands and thousands of other people. But I knew that some of my neighbors were hungry because they had been to my place and told me so. Sometimes they had food, and sometimes they didn't. Anyway, all these people were still peepin' out their windows as I walked home. I put the food in the hallway and put the trash can away. Then I went out in front of my apartment building and yelled to everybody, "Come on!" And you know, all those people who had been laughing at me came out and got some of that food. I said to myself, "This is it! Ain't no stoppin' me now!" I had done something positive, and it felt really good.

That same year we decided to have our first Thanksgiving dinner. The day before, I told everybody up and down the street to come, even though we didn't have a penny. While cleaning up our two-bedroom apartment, I found fifty cents, so I took it down to the drugstore and bought a lottery ticket. Later that day I heard the number announced on television; I couldn't believe it! I went down to the store, cashed in the ticket, and won $290. I spent $250 of it buying food at the market. That was Wednesday. The next day we served Thanksgiving dinner to thirty-nine people in the backyard. I'll never forget it. I said, "Lord, I know you're there!" The next year we served 600 people, and it just continued to grow. Within ten years we were serving Thanksgiving dinner to 45,000 people.

After that first dinner we started collecting food. Cars, trucks, buses, and even people walking by started bringing in food. Before long, everybody knew we were opening an emergency food center. Newspapers started coming; television stations started coming; radio people started coming. The media really got behind me and helped me find lots and lots of resources. All the attention brought in a lot of people who wanted to help. More black people came aboard, and I got support from the Jewish community and the white community. This older white man in the neighborhood—who hated all the blacks, hated all the whites, and hated everybody else—owned a lot of properties here. He built a room with a kitchen, bathroom, heater, and everything. Then he said to me, "Here's a place for you to meet." So he made it possible for us to get people together.

We formed a food committee and later a board that met once a month. Since we had no money I started doing public speaking to churches and different organizations, asking for donations. One day a lady came to see me and said, "My mother just died and I want to sell you her house." She knew I didn't have any money but offered me the house for $50 a month. I moved in and eventually paid it off. That became our first home.

During this time, donations were kind of slow coming in, so I decided to attend a training program at Union Memorial Hospital to learn how to care for people who had been "de-institutionalized." I didn't even know what the word meant at the time, but I took in three people with mental disabilities and became responsible for them. I took them to the hospital, got their shots, and helped them with whatever they needed. The state paid me $3,000 a month for this service, and I used the money to buy five more houses. Then I opened a bigger center in a huge building two and a half blocks away. I wanted a place where the women and children could eat together and sit around and talk at night. Early on, we called our organization the Patterson Park Emergency Food Centers. When we expanded into other areas, we changed our name to the Bea Gaddy Family Centers, Inc.

> We teach people all about self-worth. You can tell them to read books and go to school, but it doesn't mean a hill of beans until they learn to love themselves.

The first mission of our organization is to feed people who are hungry. Until you meet this need, you can't help them with anything else. Second, we teach people all about self-worth. You can tell them to read books and go to school, but it doesn't mean a hill of beans until they learn to love themselves. I lost so many years because I didn't like myself. I wasn't pushin' open any doors, because I thought I'd be thrown out. It wasn't a race thing, it was just a dumb thing. So we try to fire people up to become something. Finally, we teach them survival skills so they can become self-supporting in life. Our hope is that someday they won't need our food.

We try to meet these objectives through a number of programs. Of course, we feed everybody that comes here all day long. We set up tables outside the door that are filled with breads, meats, fruit, and so on. We never know what we are going to have because all the food is donated. But we have a regular stream of people here every day from the time we open at seven in the morning until we close at twelve midnight. If any of these people have health problems, we refer them to the Johns Hopkins Medical Center. We can get them medical assistance, mental health care, and treatment for drug and alcohol problems.

We also have a training program to help people find work. We find out which employers have jobs; then we get people ready by teaching them about self-worth, how to comb their hair, how to smile, how to dress. We even supply clothes if they need them. We have one house that is filled with clothes for jobs, funerals, church, whatever. In that same house, we have after-school tutoring for children and adult education programs in the evenings. We just finished teaching a seventy-five-year-old man how to read and write his own name. He was tired of having other people cash his checks for him. His name is Mr. Jenkins, and he's now here every day. You really need to see it to understand what we're trying to do.

Another service we have is our home-renovation program. What we do is find old houses, fix them up, and let people live in them for a year with a signed contract. We help them pay the utilities and taxes until they can take on that responsibility. These are people who get lost in the system or come to town with nowhere to go. Right now we have fourteen houses in our program. We had twenty-two, but we gave some of them away.

Last year I was operated on for cancer. I carried this disease around for twelve years, endangering my life, because I wasn't educated in health care. After that, I came up with a program to teach people how to get preventive help. These are people like me who are afraid, who are private, who don't have insurance. I'm hoping to have the best outreach program that has ever been created, because people want to live! I've just been given two big buildings. We're going to lease one to the health department and use the other one for our program. We'll work alongside organizations like the American Cancer Society.

We obviously need money to keep our programs going and help these people become totally independent. Most of our donations come from individuals and some corporations. Our budget is between $300,000 and $400,000, and we receive checks in the mail every day. Our greatest asset, however, is our 3,000 volunteers. Volunteers are very, very important to any organization. Ours are some of the smartest people in the world, and I've learned so much from them. You should see the list of people waiting to volunteer for our cancer program. We just have lots of help. We now serve more than 80,000 people a year, not including the thousands we feed on Thanksgiving Day.

We are very proud of what we do! Many of the people we have assisted are now working in banks or at other good jobs. There's a lady living down the street who was having a hard time taking care of herself and her children. She started coming here and now owns her own daycare center. She speaks well, she knows how to dress, she has finesse. She also has the prettiest little house you can imagine. I am so proud of her; I love her like my own children.

Anyway, we try to meet as many needs as we can. We are here when nobody else is; we never turn anyone away. We feed people, sleep people, clothe people, and help employ people. We even bury people! I just made out a check for $500 for the family of a young boy who was killed last week in another town. We are cooking today to make food for the funeral tonight. So we are always here for people who need us. Even people who don't need us come here because this is the place! It's really something else!

BILLY SHORE

*Billy Shore is the creator of Share Our Strength, or SOS, an orga-
nization committed to alleviating hunger now and preventing it
in the future. Billy has developed unique relationships with chefs,
restaurateurs, and companies that support the restaurant and
food-service industry. These relationships help generate new
wealth, as opposed to redistributing existing wealth, which makes
SOS more sustainable over time. Billy is also the author of*
Revolution of the Heart *and* The Cathedral Within, *two books
that encourage nonprofit organizations to generate their own
revenue. Here's his story:*

The whole time I was growing up, my father ran the district office
for our local congressman, Representative Bill Moorhead. He managed his campaigns, advised him on issues, answered his mail, and
met with anyone in Pittsburgh who wanted to see the congressman.
I grew up believing it was my dad who connected people to the help
they needed. Along the way, I decided that I, too, wanted to work in
government.

The day I got out of college, I drove down to D.C. and started
volunteering for Senator Gary Hart. Before long, I got a job answer-
ing his mail, then ended up running his office for about ten years.
After his 1984 run for the White House, I started feeling restless and
wanted to find another outlet for my desire to serve. I wasn't down
on government, because I think it plays a vital role. I just wanted to
do something that had more impact on people's lives.

One day in August of 1984, I was skimming the paper and
noticed an article about the famine in Ethiopia. It said that 200,000
people could die that summer. I was stunned! I remember having
this urgent feeling that something should be done about hunger in
the world. I also remember rather sheepishly feeling that I was having thoughts of my own for the first time in about three years. I was
very conditioned to think about what Senator Hart wanted: What
would Senator Hart think about this? What kind of press release

should we issue? And so on. So it felt good to be feeling something of my own, and I thought I should pay attention to that. As the day went on, I felt a stronger and stronger urge to commit myself to fighting hunger. Even if my contribution was small, it would be mine.

For the next few months I thought about the organization I wanted to create. The last thing I wanted to do was start another charity that spent a lot of money begging for a slice of the charitable pie. What I wanted to do was tap into new resources and create new wealth. I felt our best success would come from organizing the restaurant and food-service industry. I thought these people would feel connected to the issue because they make their livelihood from food. I didn't want them to simply donate money; I wanted them to *be* the organization. My initial concept was rather simple: Restaurants that joined up would get a seal of approval or logo to display, and we would promote that logo in ways to increase their business. I figured if 5 percent of the half million restaurants contributed $500 a year, we could raise over $10 million. We decided to call the organization Share Our Strength.

We rented a one-room basement office on Capitol Hill and incorporated as a nonprofit organization. I called Steve Wozniak, the inventor of Apple Computers, and asked him to donate a computer. He did more. He gave us a computer and a printer and sent his assistant out to train us. With Steve's computer we created lists and sent thousands of letters to chefs, restaurant owners, hotels, and franchisees. Then we waited every day for the mailman to come. Because we had a basement office, I watched his ankles pass us by every day at one-thirty. I said to my sister Debbie, who helped me start the organization, "For some reason, that guy is refusing to stop and give us our mail." I just couldn't believe that no one had responded to us.

After a while, it was clear our approach wasn't working. We were strangers asking them as strangers to get involved in our organization. It was not very appealing to anybody. What we needed were some opinion leaders in the industry to rally others to get involved. This was the theory of concentric circles we used during the Hart campaign in New Hampshire. Rather than try to persuade everyone in the state to support us, we looked for twenty-five key people with our values. This first group of twenty-five brought in the next 100, who brought in the next 1,000.

We finally got a breakthrough when Alice Waters, a prominent chef in California, sent us a check for $1,000. We asked her to write the next letter, and nearly $20,000 came in. It was clear that peer-to-peer organizing was the way to do this. So we got other chefs involved and had even more success. Along the way, we realized that many people wanted to contribute their own unique talents, as opposed to money. In other words, you or I could write out a check to SOS. We could also hand out trays at a soup kitchen. But you or I could not cook a gourmet meal at a benefit and raise $200,000. [Laughs.] But the chefs could do this, and that's how they wanted to contribute. This led to our first food-and-wine benefit with Denver's restaurant community. It was the first in a series of grassroots events that became Taste of the Nation.

Food-and-wine benefits have been around for a long time, but we do a couple of things differently. First, instead of holding one event with chefs in one city, we do it nationally—we have many chefs in many cities all doing it on the same day. The day after the event, people feel like they were part of something much bigger than themselves. So chefs in Denver who helped raise $40,000 can say they were part of an event that raised $5 million. The second thing we do is make this *their* event. We didn't start a hunger organization; we started an organization of chefs and restaurateurs who fight hunger. If you ask a chef today about his relationship with Share Our Strength, he won't say, "It's a great charity in Washington that I do a couple of events for each year." What he'll say is, "Share Our

Strength is our organization for fighting hunger." This sense of ownership keeps the event alive.

Our first full year of Taste of the Nation, we held events in eighteen cities and raised $252,000. The next year we raised $680,000, and the year after that it was $1.2 million. Today, Taste of the Nation is held in nearly 100 cities every year. About forty to sixty chefs participate in each city. They organize the event and donate the food and their time. It's interesting how they would rather spend $500 to $1,000 to be in this event than mail us a check for $100 once a year. It's because they are contributing their unique talents and bringing positive publicity to their restaurants. People from the community pay one price to get in, then graze around. They love it because they get to sample food from the best restaurants in town. The event now brings in nearly $5 million a year, and 100 percent of the proceeds go to fight hunger.

We've duplicated this same process with some of the top writers in America. It actually happened by coincidence. One day I was going through the mail and received checks from two best-selling authors: Stephen King and Sidney Sheldon. I stared at them, wondering what I could learn from this. Ultimately, I got the idea to ask the top writers in our country to contribute original stories. The response was phenomenal. The result was an anthology called *Louder Than Words,* which we sold to Vintage Books. It contains twenty-two new works from some of our best authors. One of our contributors was Anne Tyler, the Pulitzer Prize–winning novelist. With her permission, I sold her story to *Ladies Home Journal* for $3,500. If I had asked her for $3,500 over the phone, it would have been a very short conversation, yet she loved the idea of donating a story. Again, this proved my theory that people would rather contribute their unique skills and creative abilities than money.

The success we had with authors ultimately led to a national reading event. We ask writers from across the country to read from their works on the same night of the year. We do it at different bookstores and universities around the country. We now have hundreds of writers reading in dozens of cities on the same night. We call it Writers Harvest. People pay an admission fee to get in; then 100 percent of the proceeds go to local anti-hunger efforts. It's not a huge moneymaker, but it's great for awareness.

Another thing we've done with real success is build solid relationships with companies that support the restaurant and foodservice industry. Over the years, we've developed effective partnerships with Calphalon Cookware, Evion Natural Spring Water, American Express, Williams Sonoma, and others. What we do is invest a lot of time up front trying to figure out how our partnership can benefit them as much as it does us. If we fail to do this, the relationship won't sustain itself long term. So we ask a lot of questions about the mission of their business, their sales objectives, and their employee morale. We then come back with ideas for helping them meet those objectives. Our hope is to transform a philanthropic relationship into a marketing relationship. In other words, we want to create new wealth for both of us as opposed to redistributing wealth they give us. When this happens, the relationship is viable over time; we've stayed with some companies eight, nine, ten years.

Let me give you an example. Calphalon Cookware, based in Toledo, Ohio, makes high-end cookware. They first got involved with us as a sponsor of Taste of the Nation. They later approached us about co-branding a two-quart sauté pan. We ended up creating a three-way agreement. They would sell something called the Taste of the Nation pan, then pay us five dollars per unit sold for the use of our trademark. We would then send the best chefs in every community into Bloomingdale's, Macy's, or Bon Marche to do cooking demonstrations using the pan. These retailers love to have chefs visit their stores but can't always get them to do it. We were able to line them up because they are part of our organization.

Calphalon ended up selling four times as many pans as they had ever sold before. Our first royalty check was $185,000. I went to Toledo to pick it up at a company ceremony. As Dean Kasperzak, the president of Calphalon, gave me the check, he said, "I hope this check for $185,000 has a big impact on your war against hunger." As we were walking off the stage, he said in a whisper, "Boy, if you made $185,000, can you imagine what we made?" That's exactly the relationship we wanted to have with him—one driven by mutual benefit.

An interesting footnote to this story is that Calphalon was recently acquired by a large housewares company called Newell. One of the first things Newell did was offer Dean an attractive package to leave the company. Dean was the founder's son, and they didn't want the founder's family around. They also imposed some serious cost-cutting measures on the company. When they scrutinized the SOS relationship, they decided to keep it. Even though we were strangers, they felt the partnership was important to their business strategy. That was a significant test for us. Some people may have thought our partnership with Calphalon was based on a relationship with the company's owner, Dean Kasperzak. Of course, it's more important for us to have the opposite be true: To create value that holds up under scrutiny.

What we have learned from all of this is that virtually every nonprofit organization has assets it can use to generate revenue. Unfortunately, most of those organizations fail to recognize and deploy those assets on behalf of wealth creation. We've had so many organizations come to us asking for help that we actually started a for-profit consulting practice called Community Wealth Ventures. Just as the baby doctor Benjamin Spock tells new parents, "You know more than you think you do," we tell our clients, "You are worth more than you think you are." Then we help them inventory their assets and apply them to generating wealth. This is a difficult concept for some of them to accept. I have a friend in San Francisco named Jed Emerson who works with the Roberts Enterprise Development Fund. It's essentially a venture capital group for nonprofit organizations that want to start businesses. Jed starts all of his seminars by saying, "Repeat after me: Profit is good," because not everyone can say it yet; it's still a dirty word in some organizations.

I'm more convinced than ever that nonprofits of the future will not survive unless they learn to generate their own revenue. The traditional approach has been to fight for the money that's left over after individuals and corporations pay all their bills each year. This approach is not reliable or sustainable long term. It's nothing more than collecting handouts to give handouts. It's like trying to get a truck up a hill by asking passersby to give it a push on their way home from work. My approach is to create an engine to reliably and consistently get that truck up the hill. Organizations can do this by creating new wealth through products, services, partnerships, and marketing agreements. I call this type of organization a Community Wealth Enterprise. It is essentially a nonprofit for profit.

> I'm more convinced than ever that nonprofits of the future will not survive unless they learn to generate their own revenue.

To summarize, we mobilize individuals and industries, create community wealth, and distribute grants. We raise between $12 and $15 million a year for our cooking and nutrition program, grassroots events, public education, and grants to about 300 direct service providers: food banks, growth and nutrition clinics, school breakfast programs, advocacy groups, and so on. We try to fund organizations until they have accomplished their mission as opposed to being short-term funders, because success in this field takes a long time. Our long-term partnerships with businesses make us a very reliable grant maker year after year. More than half of our revenue comes from partnerships and marketing agreements; the rest comes from other activities. We have around forty staff members right now and ten more working in our for-profit consulting group. Our overall mission is to alleviate hunger now and prevent it in the long run.

My philosophy is that it takes all the sectors of society to solve our biggest problems. The government can't do it alone, and private industry can't do it alone. It really takes all of us rolling up our sleeves and getting involved. When we do, it adds new meaning to our lives. The problem is, we all want somebody else to solve these issues for us. But the big, intractable challenges of hunger, poverty, homelessness, and education will never be solved until all of us contribute our small part. So let's get involved and get it done!

PAULETTE HARDIN

Paulette Hardin is one of the original founders of SHARE (Self Help And Resource Exchange). SHARE helps more than 150,000 families get more for their food dollars. Each family pays $14 a month, donates two hours of time, then receives between $25 and $30 worth of groceries. Paulette is speaking as the voice for the many people who helped start this remarkable organization.

Back in the '80s, I was a member of the Hunger Project committee in San Diego. The Hunger Project is an international organization, and we were the local chapter. Our main objective was to raise awareness in the local community and create commitment for the end of hunger. We felt that more people would get involved in solving this problem if they understood what caused it and how it could be eliminated. One of the things we did was look at all kinds of organizations that were working with hunger. We wanted to know what was available for people beyond entitlement programs and soup kitchens, which we felt fostered a dependence on charity. We encountered an organization in Los Angeles that the SHARE program was modeled after. So as much as we would like to think that we had the original idea, it was already out there.

During this time, a man named Carl Shelton attended one of our educational presentations. He was a businessman in the community and also a deacon in the Catholic Church. He was looking for new ways to address the hunger problem in San Diego; since we were doing the same thing, it was an instant marriage. It was wonderful because our group was pretty young and inexperienced in the ways of business. We thought it would be great to have a program like the one in Los Angeles, but we never could have figured out how to pull it off—it was really just wishing. Carl helped us take it from wishing to action.

In addition to business skills, Carl added a spiritual dimension. In the early '80s he met with Mother Teresa in India, and she encouraged him to go back to the United States and deal with poverty here. What she was talking about was poverty of the spirit, where someone can be on a busy street corner in New York City and still be the loneliest person in the world. Her advice was, "You don't need to go somewhere far away to have an experience; you just need to open your eyes and look around you." So Carl approached the problem of hunger from a spiritual perspective; our approach was positive social action. I believe that the synergy of our interests and how they came together was divinely inspired. I can't imagine it happening by chance.

What we all wanted to do was create an organization that was not reliant on outside funding, that could sustain itself through participation from the people who used the program. We wanted to help people who had some income but were unable to adequately meet their food needs. If you recall, the impact of corporate downsizing was starting to be felt during the '80s. A lot of people who had worked hard their whole lives now found themselves unemployed. We also had a deep recession going on. So we wanted to help people do better with the resources they had and not become objects of charity. The idea was for people to pay some money each month, then help run the program. In exchange, they would get a higher value on their grocery dollars. The idea was very attractive to us because it put people in charge of their own well-being.

We started meeting to see what we could really do. Since we

were all volunteers, we met at restaurants at 6:00 A.M.—that was the only time we could all get together. We talked about the steps we would take, who would handle each part, how we would publicize the idea, what facilities we needed, how we would handle the money, and so on. We had at least a dozen people in this initial group, many of whom were members of the Hunger Project committee. Of course, Carl was leading all these discussions—he became the first executive director of SHARE. Although he's not active in the organization today, he was our leader for a number of years.

So we created a plan for how to go forward: We would sign up people through host sites, which would be churches and community organizations. People would pay $11 in advance, and we would buy the food in bulk. We would meet the trucks, repackage everything in family portions, and have leaders from each host site pick up the food for their people. Everyone who participated in the program would be required to donate two hours each month to help with the repackaging and distribution of the food. Our goal was to give every family $40 worth of groceries for their $11 contribution.

Our first distribution was challenging—we had 7,000 people enroll in the program! This is significant because all the experts told us, "You won't get people to pay in advance for food they haven't seen." Of course, we did, to the tune of 7,000 people who put their money on the line. Distributing the food, however, was pretty comical. We bought things like pinto beans, carrots, sweet potatoes, and oranges in big truckloads, then packaged them in family-size portions. Each package had something like four pounds of pinto beans and ten pound of oranges, which is a lot of one product. So we had big volumes but not a lot of choice. Also, we packaged the food in borrowed quarters because we didn't have a warehouse. The teamsters union loaned us some folding tables and a couple of scales; other than that, we had no equipment.

We loaded the packages in the back of empty semi-trucks, then parked them in a big semicircle in Jack Murphy Stadium. We distributed the food off the back of these trucks to the host sites according to a set schedule—you know, Holy Rosary showed up at 9:00 A.M. and so on. I believe we had about seventy host organizations participate in this first distribution. They took the food back to their sites and distributed it to the families in the program. That was something we did do right. Even though we had 7,000 people in the program, it's not like they were all standing in one line trying to get their food. They were spread out over a number of locations.

The volunteer part of the program was also challenging. We required two hours of service for each food package. Well, there was no way we could possibly use 7,000 volunteers to package and distribute the food. What we did was have each host site devote a certain percentage of those hours to SHARE and the rest to the community at large. This has turned out to be a great way for people to meet their service obligation and become an integral part of their community.

The program was so successful that after a few months we rented a warehouse in San Diego and made our staff more permanent. That's when I became a paid member of SHARE. We were still lean and mean; I mean, we saved the strings from the tops of potato bags so we could use them later. [Laughs.] But we quickly went from 7,000 to 10,000 families and kept on growing. We also went from $11 to $12 per month to help cover our costs. Fifteen years later, we are only up to $14, which is pretty amazing. Unfortunately, we are not able to triple people's value anymore because of changes in the food industry—the opportunity buys just aren't there anymore. But families get $25 to $30 worth of groceries each month for their $14 payment and their two hours of service. So the basic model hasn't changed.

In the beginning, we operated as a program of the Catholic Church, under the auspices of Father Joe Carroll and the St. Vincent de Paul center. Father Joe provided the start-up money and opened doors in every direction. Because we had the credibility of the

Diocese behind us, we could go to people and say, "This is a new program of the Catholic Church we want to tell you about." As we began to add affiliates around the country, our organizational structure had to change to meet the new demands.

What's funny to me is that we did not have any kind of expansion plan but almost immediately started growing like crazy. Our growth happened the same way everything else did—through relationships. First came SHARE Virginia, which started when Lee Stuart moved to Blacksburg to do some postdoctoral work. She met Andy Morikawa, who was the director of New River Community Action. The next thing we knew, the folks from Virginia were visiting us to see how to bring SHARE to the New River Valley. We soon added affiliates in Wisconsin, New York, and New Jersey in much the same way—through relationships. As our network developed, it was clear we needed our own nonprofit organization to manage this growth. So we formed World SHARE to provide training and services to regional programs throughout the United States, and now in Mexico and Guatemala.

Initially, each group was doing their own thing locally. We quickly realized we were competing against each other for products, which sometimes drove the prices up. So we formed a central purchasing group at World SHARE in San Diego to negotiate with vendors on behalf of all the affiliates. Each affiliate is then responsible for receiving the trucks, getting the food packages together, and distributing them to their people. We now have twenty-two affiliates in the United States and more than 150,000 families in the program. Each affiliate pays 2.4 percent of its food purchases to World SHARE for the services it provides.

During our growth years, I was the queen of expansion. [Laughs.] It was my job to start up each new affiliate. I would train the members of the new staff and help them get the program running. Consequently, I've worked with most of the SHARE programs around the country in one way or another. One day I was attending a retirement dinner for the director of SHARE Wisconsin. I looked around the room at the faces of all the people and had this awakening. It was like, oh boy, do I miss this! As SHARE became more sophisticated, my job became more marketing-centered and less program-centered. I realized how much I missed our basic program, which has such an impact on the people who participate. So I applied for the job in Wisconsin and got it! I've been the director of this program for about three years. Like many of the affiliates, we are our own separate nonprofit corporation.

One of the things I love about our program is the opportunity it provides for everyday people to become leaders and make a difference. There are about 7,000 host sites around the U.S., and they're all run by volunteers. Sometimes the media likes to focus on the sad stories of our participants and how they have triumphed over their circumstances. But for me, the touching stories are about the people who come together to work for themselves and others—they always leave much bigger than when they arrive. Their strength was there all along, but it took volunteering to bring it out of them.

> The touching stories are about the people who come together to work for themselves and others—they always leave much bigger than when they arrive. Their strength was there all along, but it took volunteering to bring it out of them.

I remember one time early on, we were going late into the night because we weren't very good at packaging food yet. There was a guy there named Lenny who was a real biker. [Laughs.] He had a chain hanging down the side of his pants and looked pretty scruffy. It was getting late, and a lot of volunteers started to leave. Before long, it was just me, my mom, and Lenny. We were kind of nervous to be alone with this guy, but we really needed his help. He worked that night and came back the next day, doing hard physical work the whole time—lifting fifty-pound bags of potatoes and other things. I don't know how to describe it, but he just took charge of the situation. Well, the next month he came back again, and we were no longer afraid of Lenny—we loved him and were glad to see him. When we finished packaging, he came up to me and said, "I just want to tell you that I won't be coming back next month because I got a job." He said it with so much pride and energy. I think working with us gave him the confidence to go out and find that job.

Another time a woman showed up who would never look you in the face—her name was May. She kept coming back, and we eventually assigned her to the sign-in desk. Her job was to welcome people, then direct them into the workflow. Over the course of time you could see a big change in her demeanor. She became such an important part of the organization that people thought she was part of the paid staff. There probably aren't many places May could have shown up and made such a difference. This is a key part of the SHARE story. You need a good model and business sense, but without the legion of volunteers there is no mechanism for distribution. I believe our success has as much to do with the relationships at the host sites as it does with the food itself. If we get busy procedurally and forget about the people who make it work, it won't endure. So SHARE always focuses on relationships.

It's very important to give credit to all the people who worked so hard to make this organization happen—any one of them could have told this story. Of course, Carl Shelton had great business experience and linked us with the resources of the Catholic Diocese. Carrol Strain was the chair of our Hunger Project committee, and her husband Kelly helped line up all the host sites. David Slater joined us from the group in L.A. and was great with operations. Another guy who did a lot of the initial organizing and publicity was Peter Meisen. Then there was Lee Stewart, who had a Ph.D. in biology and is very strong in systems thinking. She helped us break the whole down into small parts so things could function smoothly. And of course, I don't want to forget my mother, Rosemary Bolton.

Some of these people are still with the organization formally, and some are not. Most of our kids are grown now, but they were all raised on SHARE. [Laughs.]

Oh, there's another wonderful gentleman I'll never forget, Charlie Gelardi, who has since passed away. Charlie was an Italian produce man who had probably forgotten more about produce then I will ever know. He was a short little man, and he always had the stump of a cigar in his mouth—he wasn't allowed to smoke for health reasons, so it was never lit. At any rate, Charlie would get on the phone and say, "Listen, these people are doing this for the community, and it's the right thing to do. You've got to give 'em the right price, and don't send 'em any junk!" So Charlie was our ambassador to the produce world; he taught us a tremendous amount about buying and handling food.

Looking back, this is such an achievement, especially for those of us on that Hunger Project committee. Early on, we all signed an enrollment card that said we were committed to end hunger, but we didn't know exactly what we would do. We were all so different, but the one thing we had in common was an abiding belief that hunger is not acceptable, and that people working together can find a solution to the problem. SHARE is a good example of what ordinary people can do when empowered by extraordinary vision and commitment.

JOSEPH GRASSI

Joseph Grassi is the founder of Skip-A-Meal, a unique approach for solving the problem of world hunger. The idea is to skip one meal each week and then donate the money you save to a local hunger organization. The approach is people-centered, not project-centered; it's a philosophy for living, not an organization. Joseph's hope is that thousands of groups will raise million of dollars to feed the hungry each year. Here's his story:

At the age of eighteen, I decided to be a missionary in the Catholic Church. I joined a group called the Maryknoll Fathers and was ordained a priest way back in 1948. The congregation wanted me to study the scriptures and teach for a while before going on a mission, so I went to Rome for three years and studied the Bible. I came back and taught for about seven years, then went to Guatemala and worked as a missionary among the Mayan Indians. I first had to learn Spanish, which wasn't too bad because I already knew Italian. Then I struggled to learn the Mayan tongue, which was hard, but eventually I could give simple instructions and sermons on Sunday.

Going to Guatemala was a great experience for me. I traveled from place to place on a horse because there were no roads. [Laughs.] Also, the Mayans are very close to nature. They live in a world where the sun is their father, the earth their mother, the moon their grandmother—and they were all speaking to them. So I had to get used to a worldview that was quite different from that of my Christian upbringing. Looking back on it, I see how much it became a part of me; they gave me a lot more than I gave them.

After three years I came back and taught at various universities—Drew University in New Jersey, Marquette in Milwaukee, and finally Santa Clara University here in California, where I stayed until my retirement. I taught in the Religious Studies Department—courses in the four gospels, the letters of Paul, and things like that. It was while I was at Santa Clara that the Skip-A-Meal idea came along. This may sound a little crazy, but one night I had a very vivid dream. In the dream, I heard someone knocking at the door, so I got out of bed. When I opened the door, I saw a lady with a child in her arms asking for something to eat. I was as scared as anything and closed the door. When I woke up the next morning, I thought, "Wow, that dream is telling me something. Maybe I need to open up the doors of my own home and share my table with the poor."

Shortly after that, I was meeting with four or five professors in

my office. We were talking about world hunger and how something needed to be done at the grassroots level. The idea came up to skip one meal each week and donate the savings to the hungry. During our fast, we would pray for the poor and make hunger relief a priority. To keep it simple, we thought we should give the money to agencies that worked directly with the hungry, places like Loaves and Fishes, the San Jose Urban Ministry, and other organizations like that.

I more or less took it over at that point. The first thing I did was send out a letter to people I knew at the university. I told them about the idea and asked them to join us. The response was very good. From that first letter, we got a nucleus of about seventy-five people involved. We all fasted one meal each week, prayed for the hungry, and donated the money to local organizations. It was a simple idea that everybody could do.

From then on, I said, "This idea needs to expand." I figured the best way to do that was through the churches, whether they were Catholic or Protestant. So I contacted people in the religious community, told them about the idea, and asked if I could speak to their congregations. Everyone I spoke to thought it was an interesting idea but didn't think I would get much support. One church I went to said, "Look, we don't want you to be disappointed; you might only get one or two people." But I said, "I believe in this idea, and I think people will respond." So I spoke to their congregation about hunger, told them about the idea, then passed out a little sign-up card. Instead of getting one or two people, I got 500! I soon learned this response was typical; everywhere I went, people got excited about doing something.

During the early years things grew pretty well. Members of our original group came from a lot of different places, and they took the idea to churches and groups outside the area. My role was to go and help them get started. The first thing I would do was speak to the group about the crisis in world hunger and help them see that it is *our* problem. It's not just something that would be nice to do; it's something we *must* do. I would tell them, "We pray, 'Give us this day our daily bread.' Now, I'm sure that if a really hungry person came along, you would share your meal with him. Well, this is a real easy way for you to do that. And it's not just your meal; you'll be a part of something much greater. If we all do this, we can change the world we live in." I just took it for granted that they were going to help.

I also emphasized the importance of fasting because it helps us understand what the poor feel. Some people would say, "I'll just send you a check." I always said, "I don't want just a check. I want you to share the crumbs you save by giving up a meal each week; I want you to feel hungry the way the poor feel hungry." Then I told them to send in whatever they wanted. I always left the amount optional so they could give without compulsion. I really wanted to develop leadership in others, not take it away from them. This allowed people to help at whatever level they wanted to. Someone of meager means could send in a small amount, and someone who gave up going to a fancy restaurant could send in quite a bit. I would get anything from one dollar a month to a hundred dollars or more, depending on the people's circumstances and their desire to help.

> I really wanted to develop leadership in others, not take it away from them.

Early on, I figured that each group should stand on its own. I continued to coordinate the group at Santa Clara, then helped these other groups set up their own organizations. They chose their own people, developed their own leadership, created their own reports, and wrote their own newsletters. They also selected the hunger organizations they supported. We encouraged them to donate to agencies that provided abundant, nutritious meals, not just slop that was left over. It was just tremendous what these groups did. It was great to get their newsletters and find out how much they were raising and where the money was going.

I always encouraged people to go and see for themselves what was happening with their money. I would tell them, "Put on your old clothes and go sit among the poor." I've done this quite a bit myself, and some funny things have happened. One time I was eating in a soup kitchen, and I guess I was kind of thin at the time. The lady next to me said, "You know, you look pretty thin; take some of mine." [Laughs.] But I made one little mistake. Somebody looked at me and said, "Hey, that's a nice wristwatch you've got there." I realized I was the only one in the place that had a watch. Another time I was eating at a place and one of the volunteers recognized me— he went to the same high school as my son. He looked at me and said, "Oh, Mr. Grassi, I never knew." In other words, he thought I was pretty bad off and needed a meal. [Laughs.]

I have no idea how many groups are doing this now because there is no central organization. This was our plan all along. We never wanted a big organization controlling things. Many nonprofit groups end up with a large part of their budget going to salaries. We insisted from the start that everybody who worked with Skip-A-Meal would be a volunteer, and that every penny given would go directly to the hungry. Even the cost of mailing is covered by people who are willing to take care of that. So that has been very important to us. It's just a simple idea we are trying to spread throughout the world. It's something we can all do outside the structure of a formal organization to exercise our personal responsibility to help the poor.

As far as I can tell, the idea has really spread. I've always been willing to speak everywhere I can, and I've publicized the idea in newsletters and magazines. Letters have come pouring in from all over the United States and different parts of the world. I send them all the instructions on how to start up the thing. My hope is that thousands of groups will raise millions of dollars for the hungry each year. There is enough food; we just need to distribute it around.

When you get right down to it, Skip-A-Meal is really just a form of volunteerism. But that's the whole secret. We have to be willing to do things without pay to create a commonwealth in the literal meaning of the word. And the best thing we can give to others is our time and concern. We've always told people that giving money is only the first step. Many of the places we support do more than just feed the hungry. They provide clothing, get them ready for jobs, and help them take their place in the world. In our newsletters we encourage people to get involved in some of these hands-on activities that will solve the hunger problem in the long run.

I think the key to making something like this work is enthusiasm for the idea. The word *enthusiasm* comes from the Greek "en thus," which means "in God." The original sense of the word was to be totally wrapped up in something you really believe in, something you are doing for others, not for yourself. I think that is so important. You have to be willing to help people, expecting nothing in return, and then leave control with them rather than controlling things yourself. This is the way to build a true commonwealth. If all of us would do this, it would go a long way to solving problems in our world. Together we can do a tremendous amount of good. That's the whole idea!

CHAPTER · 6

AIDING OUR
NEEDY

*The whole earth is my birthplace and all humans are my broth-
ers.*

KAHLIL GIBRAN

*The situation of the poor in America is our plight, our sickness.
To be deaf to their cry is to condemn ourselves.*

RABBI ABRAHAM HESCHEL

He that giveth unto the poor shall not lack.

PROVERBS 28:27

DeLois Ruffing's modest home in Washington, D.C., was falling down
around her, and she had no money to fix it up. A charitable and hard-
working woman, DeLois ran a home for the elderly, but some of the residents owed her almost a year's back rent. Although she was a certified
nurse's aid, she had not been able to find another job.

Then one day, when it seemed there was no help in sight, three
strangers knocked at her door and asked if a group of volunteers could
clean, paint, and fix up her home. Representatives from Christmas in
April, they had been given her name by a local church when they
offered to help needy people in her area. If she accepted their offer, her
home would be one of many remodeled by hundreds of volunteers
from all walks of life—accountants, attorneys, journalists, students,

homemakers—on the last Saturday in April. Astonished, DeLois thought, "Strangers just don't volunteer to help poor people!"

But on April 30 at 8:00 A.M., a dozen volunteers appeared at DeLois's door, and the renovation began. Ten hours later the house was gleaming with fresh paint, the ceiling was repaired, the plumbing was fixed, and DeLois was beaming with joy. With tears in her eyes she said, "I had two Christmases today. The first was when you people arrived. The second was a call from a temporary nursing service offering me a job. Next year, if you need help, just let me know."

Program officials took DeLois at her word and asked her to serve on their board of directors. She accepted and was soon busy recruiting volunteers, raising funds, obtaining supplies, and identifying other needy individuals. On the last Saturday of April that year, she cooked 200 pieces of chicken to feed volunteers who remodeled forty homes, all owned by elderly people who had paid their dues in life but where unable to afford expensive home repairs. DeLois's reason for serving: "Volunteers helped me when I was down. Now it's my turn."

Approximately 13 percent of the population of the United States—thirty-six million people—live in poverty. While the number of poor has not changed much in recent years, the number of people living in extreme poverty has increased. In 1997, nearly fifteen million people—41 percent of all the poor—had incomes of less than half the poverty level established by the government, which is $16,400 annually for a family of four. This represents an increase of more than 500,000 people from 1995. Many of these people are the "newly poor": they have been laid off from jobs, their working spouses have died, or they have experienced debilitating illnesses with inadequate insurance to cover the enormous costs of treatment. Within this class of poor people, approximately two million men, women, and children are homeless in America. Many of these people have jobs but are unable to afford adequate housing.

As discussed in the previous chapter, poverty and hunger go

hand in hand. Most people who live in poverty struggle to feed themselves and their children. But even those who have enough to eat often go without the basic necessities of life: shoes, clothing, blankets, bedding, and furniture. It's tough to find a job if you don't have suitable shoes and clothing. And buying gifts for your children on birthdays and holidays is generally out of the question. Poor people simply lack the things that most of us take for granted.

The elderly who are poor, in particular, have a difficult time keeping up their homes. Most of them can survive on social security, but there is no money left to paint their home, replace a roof, fix a broken porch, or repair plumbing. This past April, I had the privilege of working on a home of just such a woman. Ruth is seventy years old and lives alone. Twenty-six years ago, lightning stuck her home and did permanent damage. She and her husband replaced the house with a small Boise Cascade home. A few years later, her husband died of a heart attack. In addition, her only son was injured in an accident at work. Nonetheless, Ruth continued to volunteer in the community until she became too ill to get around. For more than twenty years, nothing had been done to her small, prefab home.

On the last Saturday of April in 1999, an army of volunteers showed up to paint her home, clean the walls, replace the carpet, mow the lawn, pull out overgrown shrubs, and weed her garden. Throughout the day, with tears in her eyes, Ruth continued to say, "No one has ever done anything like this for me before!" When we left at the end of the day, we knew this kind woman would have a comfortable and attractive home for the rest of her life. It was a remarkable experience for everyone who helped; we all benefited at least as much as Ruth did.

Here are the stories of five heroes who have devoted much of their lives to aiding the needy. Ranya Kelly has distributed thousands of pairs of shoes to poor people, enabling them to comfortably participate in school and work. Crystal Davis created the

Community Hope Center to provide food, clothing, and other necessities to the needy in Illinois, particularly those who have been devastated by personal tragedy and natural disasters. Trevor Armbrister expanded Christmas in April across America to help remodel the homes of thousands of elderly and handicapped individuals. Becky Simpson started the Cranks Creek Survival Center to bring relief to victims of the flooding that occurred along Cranks Creek in Kentucky during the past decade. And Linda Kantor spearheaded the Casa Linda project to bring together the Latino elderly and the youth in a troubled inner-city neighborhood. Together, these role models have improved the lives of millions of people. Their stories will touch your heart!

RANYA KELLY

Ranya Kelly, known as the "Shoe Lady," is the founder of the Redistribution Center in Denver, Colorado. Her organization collects thousands of pairs of shoes each year from retailers and shoe manufacturers and distributes them to the needy. Over the years, she has donated 600,000 pairs of shoes to shelters, schools, hospitals, Indian reservations, police departments, and fire departments. Her organization is 100 percent volunteer.

I received a nursing degree and worked as a nurse in California. When I moved to Colorado, I discovered that nursing didn't pay as much here, so I went to work as a manager for Avis Rent-A-Car. When our son Justin was born, my husband and I decided I would stay home and raise him, which I was lucky to do. During this time, I did various things at home to raise a little extra money.

One day I was looking for a box to ship something in, and I went behind a shoe store at a local strip mall. When I looked in the dumpster, I saw approximately 500 pairs of shoes. I didn't know what to do, so I called my husband at work. I wanted a second opinion and really trust him; even though we are separate human beings, we are a family. I said, "You won't believe what I just found! What am I going to do? Should I take 'em or what?" He said, "Go ahead and take them. They shouldn't have been thrown away in the first place." His family struggled through life, and there were times when his shoes didn't fit. The best shoes he ever had were the high-top tennis shoes the military gave him when they came through his community.

So I took the shoes out of the dumpster and loaded them into my car. When I got home, I spread them out. Some had been slashed, some had been spray painted, some were slightly used, but most of them were brand new. I handed some out to family members; then a friend told me I should take them to a local shelter. I looked at her dumbfounded and thought, geez, what's that? Well, there was a local Catholic shelter here run by a Father Woody. It was in a very dingy, drafty old school. When I got there, I saw a lady in the hallway who was pregnant. She had pants on that drug the ground and a young child standing next to her. When she walked away, I noticed she didn't have any shoes on. I turned to the priest and said, rather naively, "Why doesn't she have shoes?" I just figured everybody had shoes. He said, "We don't have any shoes that fit her." That woman changed my life.

I started going to the retail stores to ask them for the shoes they were dumping. They were a little uptight that I was taking their product out of the trash. At the time, lots of stores were throwing out merchandise that was damaged or returned. A local paper called *Westward* did an article that really helped us. It's a fairly boisterous paper—they speak their minds. The article asked why stores were dumping merchandise when people were freezing to death under our bridges. It encouraged retailers to donate merchandise to non-profits, schools, and community groups. It wasn't long before we were dealing with lots of stores in Denver: Payless, JC Penney, T.J. Maxx, and other retailers and shoe manufacturers. And when you get 4,000 to 6,000 pairs of shoes a year from one company, you can really help a lot of people.

During the same time I was searching for shoes, I was trying to find out who needed shoes in our community. It was a new experience for me. I found that the need was much greater than I had imagined. I learned that certain types of people needed certain types of shoes: people in shelters, children in schools, kids who play sports, employees in specific jobs, people on the streets. For example, high heels don't work very well for someone who is living under the bridges. They need something that will keep their feet warm. I also learned a lot about sizes. We found people in shelters who needed shoes from size fifteen to twenty. [Laughs.] These larger sizes are not available in the retail stores, so we started checking with manufacturers to see what they had. We even went to the Denver Broncos and the Nuggets, 'cause a lot of those guys have large feet. Sometimes they are willing to donate their shoes. So we identified many, many places of need and tried to find sources for those shoes.

I quickly realized how important a pair of shoes can be. Shoes are a necessity; you need them for everything you do, both indoors and outdoors. They are particularly important in employment. You have to wear certain types of shoes with specific uniforms. If you go to a job interview in a nice outfit but you have holes in your shoes, you won't get the job. It's the first impression you give somebody that makes the difference. Unfortunately, that's based on what you wear, not on who you are. If you are going for a construction job, you may need steel-toed work boots. Those are very, very expensive for anyone to purchase. But if you don't have the appropriate footwear, forget it; you're not going to get the job. So shoes can make or break you.

Anyway, we give shoes to homeless shelters, battered women shelters, schools, social workers, hospitals, and Indian reservations. We got a letter from a priest on a reservation in Window Rock, Arizona, that tells of a grandmother who walked fifty miles because she heard they were giving out shoes. We also help people referred by police departments and fire departments. If a house burns down, which usually happens in the evening when everybody's in bed, guess what? They don't have any shoes. The Red Cross is very good at helping with immediate needs, but they often only have one or two items per person.

Another thing we do is provide shoes to people who have cerebral palsy or other types of handicaps that cause their feet to be two or three sizes different. People like that have to buy two pairs of shoes to make one, and that's very expensive. One woman we helped had polio, scoliosis, and all kinds of health problems, and her feet were several sizes different. She wore flipflops all the time, even in the winter, because that was all she could afford. Her husband supported the family, but they had lots of medical bills. We gave her four pairs of shoes for various things, and it was unbelievable to see the change in her. She had never had shoes in that quantity.

Things have grown immensely over the years. In the beginning, all these shoes used to come to my house. [Laughs.] My garage was our first warehouse; then we rented storage facilities. Now we have a greenhouse that has been given to us, but it's temporary. We've purchased a piece of property and plan to build a small building. This will give our volunteers a place to sort and package things. In the past, they've had to do this while standing out in the cold.

Each year we give away thousands and thousands of pairs of shoes. These are shoes that would otherwise go to the landfill or the salvager. How many we give out each year depends on what the stores give us. Since we started, we've given away more than 600,000 pairs of shoes. And we've done all this with a volunteer staff. None of us draws a salary—not me, our board, or the people who sort and ship the shoes. I wouldn't feel good about making money on the backs of people in need. Occasionally our board says, "Hey, you really need paid staff here." It's because we've grown so much. But I feel we can do this work without a paid staff. It just takes a little more volunteerism from the community. The little bit of funding we do have comes from the Ziv Tzedakah Fund out of Maryland. Our annual budget is between $20,000 and $30,000. This covers the telephone, rent for storage units, shipping, and things like that.

Over the years we have branched out into other merchandise, but shoes are still my heart. It kills me to think that people in America actually go without shoes. At first I didn't understand why I was led in this direction, but I wanted to serve, and God provided a way to make a difference. I think he realized I needed something in my life, too. There were numerous times I wanted to quit, but something within me said I couldn't. One time we were sorting shoes when it was twelve degrees below zero, and I started complaining to the priest who was there. In fact, it was Father Woody. I said, "Father, why am I doing this? Why am I standing out here freezing my hiney off? I should just quit." He turned to me and said, "You stand in this cold for a short period to help people who actually live in it." The message was very clear. He was right. I went, "Okay, Father, I get it. I'm sorry."

> You have to believe with all your heart that you can solve any problem put in front of you, because there are lots of roadblocks along the way.

You really have to believe in what you are doing to make something like this work. You also have to believe with all your heart that you can solve any problem put in front of you, because there are lots of roadblocks along the way. Never listen to someone who says, "I don't think that can be done," because it's not true. If your cause makes this world a better place, you have to stand up and do what it takes. We need to teach this to our children. Our young people are the future of America, and they need to know they can change anything that needs to be changed. To volunteer is the most important thing we can teach them. It helps solve our problems and brings real joy into our lives. I recently visited the Holocaust Museum in Washington and saw the pile of shoes. I realized that every pair of shoes we give out means that someone gets something I've had my whole life. When a five-year-old boy with blisters on his feet tugs on your shirt and says "Thank you," it makes it all worthwhile.

CRYSTAL DAVIS

Crystal Davis is the founder of the Community Hope Center in Cottage Hills, Illinois. She and her volunteer staff offer the needy food, clothing, blankets, furniture, heaters, fans, toys, and household supplies. Equally important, they provide counseling and education to help people rise out of poverty. In the past ten years, the Community Hope Center has helped nearly 130,000 families in desperate situations. Here is Crystal's story:

My early years were very painful. I came from an alcoholic home with an abusive father. We lived in constant poverty. I sought the Lord before anybody taught me how, just to get through my childhood. I literally went out into the fields and asked God to help me survive.

When I was nineteen, I ended up homeless in Little Rock. I was panhandling, looking for a job, and living in an abandoned apartment. One day in a coffee shop, I met a person who led me to the Lord. He was part of a ministry called The Jesus Centers. I joined their group and lived by their rules. It was like joining a drug rehab center, so it was good for me.

After three years, I left their ministry and joined the Air Force. That's were I met Leameal, the man who became my husband. He had also experienced poverty, although not as bad as mine. We married and had twins. Then in 1985, we both felt God calling us to the ministry. We had overcome poverty and other problems and knew how to help people with afflictions. So the Lord laid it on our hearts to start working with poor people.

For the next two years, I went door-to-door sharing Christ with the whole town. We took every street and claimed it for God and his work. When I went to the door I never said, "My church sent me." I just said, "Jesus loves you." Then I asked if they had a prayer request. What I was doing was standing on the scriptures that say, "Wherever your feet shall trod, that have I given to you. Go out and possess the land." I'll tell you what, if I had to sit in the pews, my faith would have died a long time ago. I have a saying that goes, "If you sit in the pews, you're going to get pewy." That's just not my way of living. I felt I was called to be a missionary, and since I lived in America, that was my mission. I treated it the same as if I had been sent to Africa or Mexico. It was just plain dumb faith in God. When God says "Go," I'm not going to sit here. I'm going to go. And if that means this neighborhood, okay. [Laughs.]

> If I had to sit in the pews, my faith would have died a long time ago. I have a saying that goes, "If you sit in the pews, you're going to get pewy."

During this time, I met a lot of people with real troubles. Some were hungry, some were out of work, some were homeless. We started giving them food and supplies from our own home. We were also praying with them and helping them through their problems. Then one day the Holy Spirit told me there would be no public aid someday, and I just gasped. Remember, this was in 1987, so when I told people about it they would say, "Yeah, right." [Laughs.] But I knew we had to be prepared to reach more people. We wanted to meet as many physical needs as possible: food, clothing, blankets, heaters, cots, furniture—just a full-service crisis center. We also wanted to teach people how to rise above their poverty.

In the beginning, we visited a lot of Christian churches, trying to get them interested in our project. Most of the pastors were scared to support us. They said, "Show us first; then we'll help you." This went on for a long time, and I became discouraged. I went through seas and seas of people who were negative and doubtful. One day I said to Leameal, "This isn't working; let's just forget it." He said to me, "God wants this done. It's going to bust open." So once again we decided to step out in pure dumb faith and do it on our own. We didn't care whether a church supported us or not. God ordered it, and he would pay for it.

So we said, "Okay, we need a building." Then a miracle happened. Fire Chief John White decided to rent us the old firehouse in Cottage Hills for $100 a month. He agreed to pay for the water, two-thirds of the electric bill, and mow the grass for three years. He really believed in what we were trying to do and backed us 100 percent. It was his support and God's support that got us on our feet. Individuals started giving when they heard what we were doing. At the end of three years, we were able to buy the building for cash.

We opened the center on April 4, 1988. At the time, I didn't know how to type or use a computer or anything. I was a tenth-grade dropout, so I had no education. I decided to make a flyer telling people to come if they needed help. I got a bank to make the copies for me, then took them all over the community. I kind of did this backward because I didn't have anything to give people. But I've always believed God will provide when you're doing his work. I knew he would lay it on the hearts of people with money to support us. And that's what happened. People came by and said, "I saw this flyer at the grocery store and want to volunteer." Before long we had volunteers picking up food at grocery stores and restaurants in St Louis. We also had people donating clothes, furniture, and money. I have to give God the credit for this, because it took all the talent I had to make that ugly-looking flyer. [Laughs.] I mean, now I can type, use a computer, do mail merge, and all this other stuff. I'd never put a flyer like that out now. [Laughs.]

We helped 100 people our first month. Our first year we helped more than 5,500 people. We thought it was a real miracle because our income from donations was like $5,500. We were so excited because it cost a dollar per person to help, and we gave them so much more than a dollar's worth of stuff. We gave them food, clothing, blankets, furniture. We also tried to help them solve their problems. We even had a class every Thursday at 10:00 A.M. to help them learn to budget.

Our numbers continued to grow each year. Then in 1993 the flood hit, and we had our highest totals ever. We helped nearly 25,000 families that year. It was one of the most stressful times of my entire life. We had hundreds and hundreds of people coming down in tears from Hardin and other places on the river. They would wait in line for hours to get help. We also had companies donating whole tractor-trailer loads of stuff, like bananas, and we had to get rid of them before they went bad. It took real organizational skills to work things out. We ended up with way too many bananas and started helicoptering them to Hardin—which was totally surrounded by water. Then Hardin sent back a message saying, "Please, no more bananas!" [Laughs.] So linking the needy people with the resources was just a nightmare.

I should have taken a break after that. Most of the pantry directors in the area got severely burned out. We went through the flood, then a busy Christmas season. We all should have taken a two- or three-month sabbatical, but we just kept going. My board finally put me on a sabbatical so I could get some rest. A couple of other pantry directors were not so blessed, and their operation really suffered.

After the flood, I knew in my heart that the Hope Center had to get bigger, but I didn't see how it could happen. We just didn't have the money for a new place. We'd been saving for the Children's Hope Center to help abused kids, but we couldn't spend that money. Then in January of 1997, I get this phone call from Tom Beirmann, the president of the Bethalto School District. He tells me they want to give us the old Forest Home School for one dollar. Now this was a grade school with ten acres! It was a miracle from God. I was jumpin' up and down screamin' hallelujah. Sure enough, it was an answer to our prayers.

We had lots of people help us refurbish the school. I sent out letters asking churches and businesses to adopt a room, and they came runnin' like an army—my goodness, they really did. [Laughs.] We had twenty-five different groups take part. In fact, there was so much interest that I ran out of rooms to adopt. We now have fourteen classrooms, a gym, and a beautiful remodeled kitchen. Behind the center we have ten acres with a football field, a baseball diamond, and a basketball court. That's where we'll build our Children's Hope Center. The blueprints and zoning have already been approved. We're anxious to finish this project because child abuse is a big epidemic in our community. The longer we wait, the more kids will get hurt. But anyway, we opened in the new location in January of 1998, so that year was one of the greatest years of our entire history. It was also our tenth anniversary! We really celebrated what the Lord had done!

Right now we are helping about 15,000 families a year. We serve people from nine counties and never turn anyone down. When they get here, they come to the office and fill out the paperwork for a food order. Then they go and get all the clothes, shoes, and household items they need. We have more than fifty clothing racks in our gym, but the demand seems to be going up. Last Christmas was our busiest ever; we helped about fifty families a day; we've never seen people like that before. I think it's because the Public Aid Reform Bill eliminated aid to thousands of people. So my inspiration ten years ago was correct. God spoke it; that settles it; it's going to happen.

I think our organization is a good model to follow. We are supported totally by the local community. We get no state, federal, or United Way funding. We have nearly seventy volunteers on our staff, and no one gets paid. Many of these people are retired, and some work forty hours a week. They pick up food, sort through clothing, and provide much-needed counseling. We currently have 161 food pickups a month. Two excellent organizations in St. Louis help us line up food: Operation Food Search and the St. Louis Area Food Bank. They find it, and our volunteers pick it up and bring it back to the center. We're passing out about four tons of food a month right now. We're also getting 3,000 to 4,000 pounds of clothes donated each week. It takes ten volunteers a day to sort through things, take them to the gym and hang them up. Some of our best volunteers are people we prayed for ten years ago in our early ministry. We helped them, and now they are helping others. That's how it works.

One of our biggest events each year is our Christmas toy giveaway. We rehab all the toys that are donated during the year, then pass them out for Christmas. This year mothers started lining up at 9:45 the night before. By three in the morning there were more than twenty mothers out there in the cold. They had little stoves and candles to keep them warm. They sang Christmas carols and had a blast all night long. The next morning, I decided to videotape them and show the tape to our toy chairman. So I asked some of the mothers who'd spent the night to tell me their stories. The tape would just rip your heart out.

The first woman I talked with was in a wheelchair, and her husband was out of work. She said, "Two weeks ago I told my daughter her toys wouldn't be under the tree right away. She said to me, 'But Mommy, I've been good all year.' So right there, I knew I had to do something. That's why I'm here." The second woman had three kids, and her husband was also out of work. She was so cold she couldn't feel her feet. She was going to school and could barely make ends meet. She was there to make Christmas special for her kids. The third woman had cancer, and her husband had a broken back. She was there to get toys for her four children. After talking to these three, I was so touched I couldn't videotape anymore. I mean, these are wonderful people who are just in desperate situations. This year 450 children got four or five toys each. We passed out more than 20,000 toys in a two-week period before Christmas.

To do something like this you have to understand that God is in charge of helping the poor. I believe that with all my heart. You've got to make sure he orders it or it won't happen. And when he does, you can sit back and know he is in charge of the "poor" business. People say, "This should be in the hands of the church" or "This should be in the hands of the government." Neither, nor. I truly believe God is in charge of the Community Hope Center. He's always been in charge! I've never had to worry about money. Honestly, this is a faith ministry. I believe God ordered it, I believe he will pay for it. I've seen miracle after miracle after miracle of God's provision. But you have to do it for the right reason. If your intentions are wrong, it won't last. I've seen others do this for self-exaltation. They didn't last six months.

The blessings for doing God's work are great. Our motto at the Community Help Center is "Be a blessing and get a blessing." It may not be physical or financial, but it's definitely spiritual. I can't even number the spiritual blessings I've received. Also, the knowledge and skills I've gained are unbelievable. I'll tell you what, God will not give you a job to do, then fail to equip you with the skills. Look at me: I've learned grammar, I've learned how to spell, I've learned how to type, and I've learned how to use the computer. The need was great, and I just had to do it or die. That was my attitude. Now I'll admit, some of my first paperwork was really gross, but at the time I thought, "Wow, look what I did." [Laughs.]

My one hope now is that every city in America will open a pantry. I believe there is a great depression coming, even bigger than the one before. Actually, the Great Depression never went away; it was just blanketed by public aid. But public assistance was never intended to last this long, and it's made families dependent on the government. Now that it's going away, the need will be greater than ever before. It's time to take back our responsibilities as citizens. We need to feel compassion for the poor, and most important, help them climb out of their poverty. I would encourage anyone with an inkling to help to get started right away. It's what we should all be doing.

T R E V O R   A R M B R I S T E R

Trevor Armbrister is the founder of Christmas in April of Washington, D.C., and a cofounder of Christmas in April USA. The national organization—comprised of 250 affiliates in all fifty states—brings together 220,000 volunteers on the last Saturday of April each year to repair the homes of more than 6,600 needy families. Christmas in April is one of the most successful programs in the country at uniting people from every race, color, and creed behind a common goal: to improve the homes of our poor, elderly, and handicapped neighbors.

I've been writing for *Reader's Digest* since 1970. In 1982, our bureau chief, Bill Schulz, suggested I do a story on volunteerism. This was during the Reagan years when some people felt volunteerism was decaying. Bill's attitude was, "That's not true; people are still nifty in America." So I did some research and picked four people to feature in the story.

One of the guys I chose was Bobby Trimble of Midland, Texas, who had started something called Christmas in April. What I found least appealing about this story was having to go to Midland, Texas, on a weekend. I was a bachelor at the time and much preferred assignments in places like San Francisco. But I ended up in Midland and met Bobby on Friday night. He kept telling me that thousands of volunteers would show up the next day to repair the homes of needy people all over the city. Sure enough, 3,000 people of all colors, races, religions, and creeds united the next morning with one common purpose: to make their neighbors' homes safer and more comfortable. No one was browbeating anyone. It was a quiet sense of, "Let's get the job done."

They worked on eighty-four homes that day. The beneficiaries were black, white, Hispanic—people who had paid their dues but were suffering for whatever reason. It was one of the most marvelous things I had ever seen: People putting aside whatever differences may separate them for a common purpose. And they were doing it joyfully. In the middle of the day they had a big lunch and everyone sat together—you could feel the camaraderie. When they finished, they went back to work until the job was done. Throughout the day, I wandered around with my notepad and tape recorder, trying to get the story. It was a transforming experience for me. I had my epiphany that day.

Most of my stories only stay with me for a day or so until they are shipped off to the editor and I get a new assignment. In this case, I couldn't stop thinking about what I had seen in Midland, Texas. It was such a sensible idea. I started asking, "Why can't we do the same thing in Washington?" I was convinced people would respond if we asked in the right way. Although I'd lived here since 1965, I had never become involved in a community activity. It was past time for me to start.

You've probably found that being really dumb is sometimes an advantage in life. Well, if I had had any idea how difficult it would be to start one of these things, I'm sure I would have flinched and said, "Let someone else handle it." But I enlisted two friends to help, Tom Kennelly and Tom Henderson, and we plunged forward. Our first objective was to recruit various churches in the area and make this an interfaith effort. We really wanted it to be totally inclusive. Kennelly is a good Irish Catholic and I'm Episcopalian. We figured if we could get the Mackerel Snappers and Whiskopalians together, we'd be off to a good start. [Chuckles.]

Initially, my vestry at St. Columba's Episcopal was somewhat skeptical. "What criteria are you going to use to select the homes?" "How are you going to raise the money?" "How are you going to attract hundreds of volunteers when the most we've ever assembled for a project is a hundred?" "Aren't you biting off more than you can chew?" I learned a lot about volunteering real fast. In retrospect, their questions were helpful because they forced us to address some difficult problems early in the game.

By the end of that year, we had enlisted support from a half-dozen churches in the area. Next, we set out to select the homes we would try to repair. Our first requirement was that the occupants had to own the home. We didn't want to make free repairs only to have some slumlord raise the rent. Then we determined that the homeowner should be poor, elderly, or handicapped. Finally, we agreed the condition of the home had to pose a health hazard or cause discomfort to the occupants. With help from our churches, community leaders, and city officials, we identified eighteen homes to repair that coming April.

Our goal that first year was to attract 300 volunteers and raise $10,000 for materials, so I started talkin' up a good game. I relied heavily on my own network of friends and associates. There used to be a bar here called the Class Reunion, which was a favorite of journalists and staff during the Reagan White House. I would go there and shanghai colleagues of mine, saying, "Sober up and come out and help." I twisted so many arms I got the nickname of Armtwister instead of Armbrister. I found lots of people to help, but most of them were klutzes with home repairs, just like me. Eventually I gained the support of the local trade unions, which both surprised and delighted us. They conducted a walk-through of the eighteen homes early that spring to determine what each needed, how much the materials would cost, and how long the work would take.

We decided to hold the event the last Saturday of April. The weather in Washington was horrible that whole week. We committed to persevere regardless of what April 30 brought. Fortunately, the weather was perfect on Saturday. What happened that day was amazing; it bordered on being a miracle. We raised $11,000 for supplies, had 325 volunteers show up, and renovated all eighteen homes. We got very nice stories in the *Washington Post* and the *Washington Times*. So Christmas in April of Washington, D.C., was off and running.

The second year, we did thirty-six homes with the help of 500 to 600 volunteers. We got some resistance that year from a few people who were suspicious of what we were doing. It was like, who are these honkies? We were accused of fronting for a real-estate company that was going to grab up the properties. Our actions disproved those accusations. People saw we were sincere, and we've never had barriers like that since. Today, Christmas in April is known as a pretty nifty operation in this community.

The first thing we do when we go to a property is remove any trash. Some people don't know how to throw things away. I'm a good example of that; I never met a piece of paper I didn't want to keep forever. So we try to have volunteers with trucks standing by to haul things away. Then we start on the structural repairs. We patch walls, paint, replace stairs, fix decks and porches, and even repair or replace roofs. About half the homes in D.C. need new roofs. Our insurance won't let us do roofs, so we either pay to have it done or get professionals to donate the service. Again, we've been very successful at twisting arms, and we get about half our roofing work done for free.

I've got to tell you, I have absolutely zero talent or ability with any of this stuff. I don't know the difference between a dead line and a plumb line. If I have any skill at all, it's in telling people what we are doing, rounding up the volunteers, and encouraging them with a pat on the back. Actually, it's not that hard to find volunteers. We get great support from churches, schools, and colleges. Some schools even give credit for volunteerism. Then once people do this, they all want to do it again. It's one day out of the year they can give to their community, and in the course of giving, they get a real emotional payback. We now get between 3,000 and 4,000 volunteers each year, and we renovate nearly a hundred facilities, including houses, community centers, and schools. We've renovated more than a thousand homes in D.C. since we began in 1983.

In 1988 I was persuaded to expand the organization nationally. I thought we needed one more year to grow, but Patty Johnson, the executive director I hired in 1984, convinced me we needed a national organization with a presence in Washington, D.C., to support communities all over the country. She was right; my hesitancy was wrong. So six of us as cofounders started Christmas in April USA in September of that year. It was myself and Patty plus Bobby Trimble, Steve Winchell, Bob Macauley, and John McMeel. These people are fantastic! We had no money, so Steve loaned the organization $12,000. We knew of a handful of other similar programs in the country, so we linked up with them and offered our support. Then requests for information on how to start this thing began flooding in from everywhere. It's just amazing how it has spread! Most of our affiliates use the name Christmas in April.

Our relationship with these affiliates is a lot like a franchiser to a franchisee. We have an extensive training program that teaches them how to set up Christmas in April in their city. We provide fund-raising assistance, a national insurance program, ongoing support, and a national conference each year with great speakers and workshops. We had about a thousand people show up last year because it was our tenth anniversary. Our affiliates pay a very small fee—two cents for every dollar they raise—to cover the support we provide. We now have about 250 affiliates in all fifty states. Each year on the last Saturday in April, we have about 220,000 volunteers renovate more than 6,600 homes and other facilities across America. Everyone's reaction to the program has been just like ours. It unites diverse communities by getting people together behind a common good.

We fund the national organization with individual contributions, corporate sponsorships, and special events. That first year, our budget was minuscule; now it's over a million dollars. Our foremost national sponsor is the Home Depot out of Atlanta. They donate tons of materials and are fantastic to work with—a real forward-looking organization. We've also had support from teams in the NFL. The commissioner, Paul Tagliabue, was one of our house captains in the early days; he has a real affinity for Christmas in April. I also recruited his wife, Chan, to serve on our national board.

Overall, our supporters are happy to help because we're a mean, lean, clean organization. We really do get a big bang for every buck.

I would say the most important key to our success has been teamwork. Rome wasn't built in a day, and I didn't do this by myself. Nothing worthwhile is ever done by one person. My wife will tell you I work hard, but I'm not very organized. If other people had not spotted that weakness and picked up the slack [laughs], this thing would not have happened. Also, I think it's important to say when you are wrong. I told you I was wrong about launching the national organization. I was also wrong about funding a national headquarters. Three years ago, my colleagues wanted to buy a home for $650,000. I thought our money should be used to help the people, not create a shrine for ourselves. Well, I got outvoted. As it turned out, we found some benefactors who paid off the mortgage. We now have a great headquarters in the nation's capital, we can serve our affiliates better, and we can dedicate all our resources to helping the needy. Working together cooperatively is so important. Here's another example. I've written four books during my career. The two I wrote with other people hit the *New York Times* bestseller list; the two I wrote by myself did not. The truth is, we're stronger when we work together.

> The most important key to our success has been teamwork. Rome wasn't built in a day, and I didn't do this by myself. Nothing worthwhile is ever done by one person.

Patty Johnson is now the president and CEO of Christmas in April USA, and she is superb! I retired from the active board in November of '97 after fifteen years of service. I felt it was time to bring new blood into the organization. The thing I'll always remember is the payback I received when I least expected it. One year we were remodeling the home of an elderly white couple in a nice section of D.C. They seemed well-to-do, so I kept asking myself, "What are we doing here?" Then I found out the husband had some rare disease that his insurance wasn't paying for. His illness was draining their resources, and they were barely surviving. At the end of the day, the wife said to me, "I want to pay you." I told her, "We don't do this for money." She said, "I know you don't take money, but I want to give you a gift." It turned out to be a family Bible that she insisted I take. My fiancée was with me, and we used that Bible at our wedding. How do you put a price tag on that?

Anyway, the whole thing has just been marvelous. I've learned a lesson I probably should have learned long ago: It is far better to give than to receive. And it was such an accidental discovery! If my bureau chief had asked someone else to do the story on volunteers, I would not have known about this. But he didn't; he asked me. Here I was hating the fact that I was wasting a weekend in small-town Texas where nobody drinks anything stronger than apple juice, and it totally changed my life.

BECKY SIMPSON

Becky Simpson is the founder of Cranks Creek Survival Center in Noah's Hollow, Kentucky. She started the center after three major floods totally devastated the area. During the past sixteen years, her organization has provided food, clothing, shoes, blankets, and improved housing to thousands of families living in poverty. She says:

I was born and raised on Cranks Creek. There's a lot of little Hollows around here and all of 'em's got names. Ours is called Noah's Hollow—it was named after my grandfather. We was raised as hard as you can be raised. Seven of us lived in a little two-room house. My dad worked for a dollar and a half a day. My mother plowed gardens and that sort of thing. I dropped out of school in third grade 'cause we couldn't afford no shoes—it was real cold that winter. So we grew up without a lot of things. I guess you don't miss somethin' if you never had it. But watchin' my mother suffer was the hardest thing for me.

When I was pretty young I decided that someday I would help poor people. I just didn't think no one should have to go without the basic things of life: food, shoes, clothes, shelter. As I got older, I started helpin' out family, friends, and anyone in need. I would just give 'em anything I had. I've actually given away my last pair of shoes. [Laughs.] I'd just take a chance I'd get more, and I always would. I really do love people with a passion, and I hate human suffering. I've been that way since I can remember.

Back in '77 we had three big floods. They had strip-mined the mountains, and they just washed off into the valley. Big trees and rocks and stuff came right on down. About four and a half miles of the area was totally demolished. We'd had little floods before—we called 'em tides—but nothing like we was havin' then. A lot of people that was raised as poor as I was had got up to middle-class living. After the floods they came back down to nothin'. I kept thinkin', Lord, somebody's gotta do somethin'.

> I've actually given away my last pair of shoes. I'd just take a chance I'd get more, and I always would.

At the time, I evaluated my life, and it was a dark spot. I couldn't do paperwork 'cause I had no education. I couldn't do manual labor 'cause I had a bad back injury. What happened was just a miracle. I started listenin' to the radio and readin' every paper I could get my hands on. Gradually I started workin' out in the public, which scared me to death. Me and the circuit judge's wife started lobbying officials in Frankfort to get help for Harlan County. The federal government had flood repair money, but you had to get it from the state. Eventually we got some, but it didn't come to Cranks Creek. We're like eighteen miles out of the city. We had no bridges left, and none was gettin' built. We had no wells, and none was gettin' drilled. We also needed the creek dredged and stretched out. We'd get like a million dollars, but they never included this place up here.

So in '82 I decided I was going to quit. Then one day a friend and I was sittin' on the mountain crying, lookin' at some strip mines. I told her I was gonna quit workin', and she said, "Lord, you can't do that, you've come too far." I said, "Well, what else can I do? I can't climb up to their level, and they ain't comin' down to mine." And she said, "Why don't you make a little place of your own. I'll even name it for you. You can call it Cranks Creek Survival Center." Well, that was news to me. Her name was Mary Bebe, and she's one of the sweetest people I ever knowed. She planted the seed of me doin' somethin' on my own after tryin' to get help for five years.

I wanted to help as many people as I could, but I felt it would be worth it even if I only helped a few. I just didn't want no one bein' hungry and cold in the winter, and I didn't want no children droppin' out a school 'cause they ain't got shoes. At that time, we didn't have no buildings on the property, so I just worked out of my living room. Then my husband, Bobby, bolted a little room together out here so I could use the phone in peace and quiet. Bobby's first cousin gave me $25 to put an electric meter on the building. Another organization was goin' out of business and gave us what they had left over. It ended up being $1,700 worth of stuff, which went a long way to get this place ready.

Before I opened up, I had to incorporate and get some tax numbers. I had some friends at Legal Services help me do that. Then I put the word out I was startin' a survival center. I ain't good about askin' for myself, but I'm pretty good about askin' for other people. I just told folks to bring in things they didn't need anymore whenever they cleaned out their closets. Before long we was gettin' clothes, shoes, curtains, bedspreads, and even carpet people had taken up. It just pleased me to death. The shoes especially meant so much to me. So that's how it all got started.

I can't tell you the number of people we've helped over the years, but it's into the thousands. Those who come to the center take whatever they need. We're three miles from the Virginia line, so people up there come on down, which they're welcome to do. Then we go out to four counties around here and Harlan. We've got our hands full tryin' to cover that whole area. We don't have money for a paid staff or anything like that—it's just me, family members, and other volunteers. Bobby helps as much as he can, but he lost his sight in '62. He goes out with drivers and picks up the stuff people donate. The center is totally funded through donations. The biggest donation we ever got came from Community Trust outta Knoxville. We bought a little piece of property to build a children's home on. As far as I knowed, there's never been one in this county. But it was swampy bottomland, so Community Trust donated $41,000 to fill it in, do the landscaping, that sort of thing. We're hopin' to get that center open this year.

Of course, our busiest time of the year is Christmas. We started doin' it back in '83 and been doin' it ever since. That first one was a high point in my life, 'cause growin' up we had very little at Christmas. What we do is mail out about 1,200 letters to people on our mailing list. I been savin' up names since back in '77. I don't come right out and ask for money; I just tell 'em we'd appreciate anything they want to donate. They send back money and all kinds of things. We buy ham and turkey and pack the building full of clothing. Everybody that comes gets a food basket and anything else they need. We had 650 families come out last year. It was the first time we had enough meat to last through the whole giveaway. We also had 700 new blankets, so each family got one. A church up in Worthington, Ohio, has been helpin' us out with this for the past five years. It's called the Saint Michael's Youth Ministry. In October we start collectin' the names of children who need shoes, then send the names up to them. We try to do two schools each year. Saint Michael's then brings down 1,000 pairs of shoes, blankets, and a U-Haul full of food. The man's name is Bob Moraine, and he's a real saint.

Another thing we have is a little housing project. We find people that live in small places and add on to their homes. It's all done with volunteers. Most of 'em come from colleges and churches. Each person that comes brings $60; we keep $10 to pay the bills, then put $50 into somebody's house. We just did three little houses. They were all two rooms, so the children had to sleep on the floor. Our volunteers went out, bought the materials, and added the extra rooms. All the groups that come here are great! For years they had to rough it when they came to work, but now we've got a nice place for 'em to stay and cook their meals. Over the years we have built or added on to more than 500 homes. It goes to show you can really do a lot if you work together.

Doin' this kind of work is real touching to me. One time the *Courier Journal* from Louisville came up here to do a story. At the time, I was pickin' up surplus food at Kroegers and takin' it to people's homes. I went to the house of a man I knowed from school—what little I went. They was living in a little mining shack; it was made of cinder block and had no windows. It was dark as pitch inside, and they had two small children. I dropped off some bread and donuts and was walking back to my car. It felt like someone was watching me, so I turned around and saw their five-year-old girl Priscilla standin' there. I went back and talked with her, and it was very touching. I asked her if she hurt livin' in that house, and she said, "Yeah." Then I asked her if she'd like to live better, and she said, "Yeah." It's hard to imagine unless you see it. I hate dark houses 'cause my dad grew up in one. He developed cataracts, and the doctor said it was 'cause he seldom saw daylight. It made me feel real sorry for Priscilla livin' in that dark house. Well, the *Courier Journal* used her in their article, and before long she had everything she wanted. I wish I could get more stories out like that 'cause it does help. Most people just don't understand the need.

My advice to others is this: If you see a need, don't turn your back on it, 'cause it ain't gonna go away. As I said before, I just love people with a passion, and I hate human suffering. I wish more people would get involved in helpin' the poor. If I can do it, anybody

in the world can do it! You just have to put one foot in front of the
other. I believe everyone can and should try to make a difference.

LINDA KANTOR

*Linda Kantor is the founder of Casa Linda, a neighborhood cen-
ter in New Haven, Connecticut, that brings in the elderly from a
senior housing project to teach their arts, culture, and skills to
neighborhood youth in after-school and summer programs.
Skills being taught at the center include music, cooking, sewing,
doll-making, language, child care, gardening, jewelry-making,
and many other employable skills. These cultural and multigen-
erational exchanges have revitalized the neighborhood and
restored pride to a once-troubled community. Here's Linda's
story:*

I got involved with senior housing when I was asked to serve as Chair
of Arts and Design for a high-rise project in New Haven. It was a
twenty-one-story building with 217 units for the elderly. At the time,
the routine was that seniors were being cubbyholed in apartments,
then forgotten about. These projects were typically sponsored by a
nonprofit organization and funded with a low-interest government
mortgage. The loan was paid back over many years with the rents of
the senior citizens who moved into the project. Being five foot two—
the same height as many of our senior clients—I became an advo-
cate for the elderly. We worked hard to get adequate staffing,
programming, and other services for the residents.

This first project was such a success that I was asked to serve as
building chair for a second project. At the time, we had about 3,000
units of senior housing in our city, but only three of these were
occupied by Latinos. Cultural and language barriers made it very
difficult for Latino elderly to complete an application and adjust to
a new housing environment. So this new project was 105 units
designed specifically for Latinos. The project was sponsored by a

Catholic church in the neighborhood and funded with a mortgage from the government. Cesar Pelli, a famous architect from Argentina who was dean of architecture at Yale at the time, agreed to design the building. Normally, architects get 15 percent of the building costs. Caesar agreed to do it for 3.5 percent, the amount allowed by the government, so he basically donated his time.

The building turned out to be superb! Each floor is a neighborhood rather than a group of apartments. People in the community were quite excited about it. Our first resident moved in before we had a superintendent or staff. She was a grandmother with thirty-seven grandchildren. Someone asked her if she was afraid to move into an empty apartment building by herself. Her reply was, "I've always wanted to live in a big house." She was a very gutsy lady. After she moved in, the building filled up immediately. We named it Casa Otoñal, which means Autumn House.

Shortly after the project opened, New Haven hit rock bottom. We had shootings, drug traffic, fires, and lots of destruction. Unfortunately, Casa Otoñal is located in one of the poorest neighborhoods in the city. Across the street was a small factory for fabricating tombstones. It was a little two-story house and some sheds. The owner had died, and the place had became a dump and drug refuge. It was brought to our attention by the New Haven Preservation Trust. They felt it had historical architecture and hoped Casa Otoñal could do something with it. So I went to the property with our president and executive director, and we walked through the house. They saw no hope for the place and thought it should be demolished. It was not only an eyesore, it was also dangerous. The yard was totally overgrown, the sidewalk was broken up, and there were needles and garbage all over the place. It hadn't been that bad when we started our apartment building, but it was becoming worse and worse—as was the neighborhood.

A while later I was sitting at breakfast with my husband, and we were talking about the future. He asked me, "Is there something you really want to do?" I said, "Absolutely." And he said, "What is it?" I said, "I want to renovate that house across the street from Casa Otoñal." He didn't say, "You can't do that" or "That will never work." What he said was, "If you want to do something like that, you should do it." Right at that point, I knew it would work. And while some wives get jewelry and furs from their husbands as gifts, I got a Ford pickup truck. The project was obviously important to me, and I had his full support. So I took what money I had, negotiated with the real-estate people, and bought the house.

I guess my motivation for doing this came from two places. First, my mother was the eldest of seven children and grew up in a poor section of Washington, D.C. Near her home was a settlement house where people would congregate—both old and young. It was there she learned to sew, gained confidence to finish high school, and developed skills that enabled her to be employed. Even in her old age and sickest times, she remembered this settlement house as one of the highlights of her life.

My second source of inspiration was an old woman I met in Jerusalem while my husband was on sabbatical from Yale. Her name was Myriam Mendilow, and she was committed to helping the poorest of the poor. She believed that all human beings, especially the elderly, need to wake up each morning with a purpose. Her motto was "To be is to do." What she did was organize workshops to help people improve their lives. She would ask everyone she met, "What can you do?" If they said, "Well, I can weave baskets," she would say, "Okay, you are going to teach basket-weaving." So everyone was working together and learning new skills. She even had the elderly cook meals for other elderly and take them to their homes. Some of these people could barely walk, but they came every day. And all of this happened in the poorest neighborhood in the city; it was just up the hill from the Damascus gate of the old city. Myriam always said, "If you want to help the poor, you have to go where they are; you can't expect them to come to you."

So my thought was to build a center where the elderly from Casa Otoñal could come and teach their culture and skills to the community. The first thing I had to do was clean up the property. I went to a halfway house in the area and arranged to have some of the residents help me. I would pick them up in my truck in the morning, provide lunch, then take them back at night. I paid them by putting money directly into each man's personal account. Before long, everyone in the halfway house was volunteering to work; they would line up in the morning hoping to be chosen; there were always more people than I could ever use. So sometimes I had the same people, and sometimes I had different people.

> If you want to help the poor, you have to go where they are; you can't expect them to come to you.

I worked right alongside the men every day. I taught them different skills I had learned during my construction experience; they taught me skills as well. We put a chainlink fence around the property, cleaned up the yard, repaired windows, did brickwork, put in insulation, fixed the stairs, refinished the banisters, and painted the place. We tried to save everything of historic value. We also added all new utilities: lighting, telephone, heating, air conditioning, and ceiling fans. We even added a porch in the backyard so the elderly could go outside and sit in the sun. Everyone worked hard every day.

As time went on, the men started eating lunch with the elderly at Casa Otoñal. They would sit at the tables, and the elderly would serve them. As it turned out, a grandparent of one of these men was living at Casa. It wasn't long until the elderly were taking real pride in the reconstruction of this little house. They would show up in the mornings and help in any way they could. Then people from the neighborhood started coming out to cheer us on. I put a sign on the chainlink fence telling people we were building a neighborhood house, so everyone knew what we were doing. They would come by and say, "What can I do to help?" "Do you want some flowers to plant?" Even the kids got excited about it. They would ride around the corner on their bikes and yell, "Hey lady, you're doin' a good job!" [Laughs.]

One day a very tall street person walked in the front door while we were working. He wore diamond rings and gold chains around his neck. All the sawing and hammering suddenly stopped. My workers had all been criminals themselves, but they seemed real nervous. The guy looked down at me and said, "What's this gonna be?" I said, "It's a neighborhood center where children and old people can get together." He said, "Oh yeah?" Then he started scoping out the place to see what might be profitable. When he smiled I noticed that he had a diamond in his front tooth, so I said to him, "That's a nice diamond. If you have anything you can contribute to our project, we would appreciate it." He said, "Sure," then went away. We never saw that man again. I realized that even the hardest criminals care about grandfathers, grandmothers, and children—they simply left us alone.

While we were renovating the house, everyone referred to it as the house across the street. When it was ready for occupancy, the elderly named it Casa Linda. In Spanish, *Linda* means beautiful, so it was the Beautiful House. Since Linda is also my name, they started calling me "Linda Two Times"—it was really nice.

As I said, my hope was to provide a place for the elderly to go each day. I wanted them to get up, get dressed, and walk across the street just like they were going to work. That's exactly what happened. One of the first things they did was make dolls. The men would cut out the patterns and fabrics, and the women would make elegant dresses, trousers, and shirts. They also embroidered wonderful faces on these dolls. Some of them were three feet tall! We started donating them to children in the hospital who had contagious diseases. Because of their illnesses, these kids were not allowed to play with the usual hospital toys. We called them "A Pal in Bed." We also gave dolls to the police department so they could give them out to children who had experienced trauma: a fire, a disaster, or a family dispute. In addition, Yale had a clinic for domestic violence and needed dolls for role-playing. So the elderly made entire families of dolls—grandparents, parents, and children—in all different skin colors for that program. We sold some of these dolls to help pay for the materials.

It wasn't long until a million things were happening in that little house. One of our objectives was to provide a vehicle for the elderly to pass on their heritage, so we started after-school programs from 2:30 to 5:00 P.M. We began teaching doll-making, sewing, music, cooking, jewelry-making, gardening, knitting, and quilt-making. The older men taught the kids how to make dominoes in a carpentry class, and we held tournaments with old and young combined. We taught classes in English and added a new parent program. Attendance was always like 300 percent because the kids would bring their siblings, aunts, fathers, and mothers. I hate to say it was a party because that sounds like sheer recreation, but it really was a party of learning.

I quickly realized it was not what we were doing that mattered, but what was happening while we were doing it. While you're teaching cooking there is conversation; while you're reading a story there's an arm around a shoulder; while you're gardening, you're out in the dirt together. It's that unspoken communication between a young person and a role model that makes the difference. And in this case, the elderly were a promise of a future. Many of the young people in this neighborhood felt they would die before they turned twenty—it was the shootings and all the violence. These old folks were proof you could survive—and not only survive but also learn skills to improve your life. All this occurs while the old and young are working on projects together. It's analogous to the old-time quilting bees where whole families sat around quilting and talking. So the conversation that happens during the activities is the real value of our program.

The great reward of this work is seeing the kids make progress. Some of the children that come here are the sole cooks in their families. They often show up with a bottle of Coke and a bag of potato chips. After taking our gardening and cooking classes, they start making and eating salads. It's also exciting to see them take responsibility for their future. I asked a teenage girl in our jewelry class if she had a boyfriend. She told me she did. Then I asked her if she had any children, which a lot of them do. She looked at me and said, "What are you talkin' about, Linda? I work at Kentucky Fried Chicken. I can't support a child now!" We're trying to teach them the serious consequences of teenage pregnancy, so maybe our message is getting across.

As I mentioned, I bought the building myself and paid for the renovation. Since then, our programs have become so successful that we've expanded them. We tore down the old sheds in the back and built a larger community center for the neighborhood. It was all built by volunteers. We now have expanded programs every day and a summer camp every summer. The operation is currently funded with grants from community foundations, private contributions, and some fund-raising events. And it all started from this little house.

The transformation of the neighborhood has been the real miracle. People now walk down the streets and greet each other. A neighborhood group meets regularly in the center. We've had weddings, baby showers, and rehearsals for the marching majorettes. We've even had a parade. The man who owns the railing factory nearby donated his flatbed truck, and the cemetery donated huge wreaths. We've also planted an entire hillside for the Special Olympics here in New Haven. The old and young grew the plants together, then planted the Olympic logo right on the hill. It seems to be spreading down the street, person by person, house by house. People who haven't talked with each other in twenty years are now working together. Every time my husband and I go walking downtown, someone zooms by and yells out, "Hi, Linda." My husband always says, "Who's that?" I say, "One of my people."

I think several things help this kind of work succeed. First, learn to constantly recycle. If you go to the dump, it will open your eyes to all the wonderful things people throw away. The trick is to get these items before they end up in the dump. Office supply companies, furniture stores, various manufacturers, consignment shops, bakeries, and restaurants all dispose of surplus goods in one way or another. We got all of our conference tables, chairs, bookcases, and filing cabinets from a company that was remodeling. And you can always find used computers because people are constantly upgrading. So look around your community for people who can contribute recyclable goods. This keeps your costs down.

Second, when you're raising money, look inside your own neighborhood first. Try to identify individuals and businesses that directly benefit from your work. These are the people most likely to contribute. Many fund-raisers look for money outside their area, and it doesn't work very well—they think people will donate because the cause is good. Unfortunately, this is not the case. To succeed, you have to partner up with people who have the greatest stake in your own community. This is true for finding both money and volunteers.

Finally, you have to give credit to everyone who participates. When I hear people taking tours around our center, they never talk about Linda. They say things like, "We did this" and "This is our program." They feel a great sense of ownership, which is important for the organization to survive. So you have to clone yourself. If other people don't buy into your vision, you have no continuity. In fact, I think you need to purposely step back after a few years to see if the organization can carry on without you. If not, you have a lot more recruiting to do.

Oh, there's one last thing. Buy yourself a truck. [Laughs.]

CHAPTER 7

BUILDING A
SUCCESSFUL
NONPROFIT
ORGANIZATION

In past decades, nonprofit institutions were almost extraneous to a society dominated by government programs and behemoth corporations. Many people believed that the role of nonprofit organizations was to supplement existing government programs. Today, we understand that the government's ability to solve our problems is limited, and consequently community-service organizations are becoming central to our society—they address our toughest social ills and enable us to fulfill our civic responsibilities in America.

Unfortunately, the failure rate in the charity world is high. Nonprofit organizations don't declare bankruptcy the way for-profit companies do, and they don't always go out of business. Instead, they fail to achieve the objectives for which they were established. Many are full of big-hearted people who lack leadership and organizational skills. Others thrash around on the treadmill of never-ending fund-raising, doing as much as they can with whatever they raise each year. Some fizzle out from fatigue as the dream that fuels their passion takes too long to materialize.

In this final chapter, I summarize eight keys to building a successful nonprofit organization. I gleaned these concepts from studying dozens of organizations, including the ones featured in this book. While these principles were derived from the nonprofit arena, I believe that any organization can benefit from these sound practices. After all, the main difference between nonprofit and for-profit organizations is an accounting detail—both have missions, both need leadership, both have products or services, and both have customers they serve. Although numerous management concepts could be reviewed here, the following are particularly critical to community-service organizations. Notice that these keys are *things you do,* not personality traits.

KEY 1: PROCLAIM YOUR PASSION

The business world belongs to people with passion! Like concentric circles from a rock thrown into a pond, passion ripples forward, affecting everyone it touches. It draws people to the idea; it attracts members to the team; it entices customers to buy; it enables an average bunch of folks to achieve incredible results. Passion is infectious! Passion is captivating! Passion is power! It isn't possible to get a new business off the ground without a healthy dose of passion.

Passion is even more important in the nonprofit world because the incentives common to businesses are not always available: salaries, bonuses, and return on investment. While the for-profit entrepreneur has passion *plus* financial rewards, the social entrepreneur has only the passion to solve a difficult problem—at least in the beginning. The fact is, without an unfathomable amount of enthusiasm for the cause, a new social venture is never going to succeed.

Overwhelming passion does two things for the aspiring social entrepreneur. First, it is the foundation for perseverance. If you really believe in your cause, you'll have the strength to work long hours, solve problems that arise, and keep going during formidable adversity. The obstacles to launching a social enterprise are just too great to surmount without a real fervor to make it happen. Second, passion is the great orator that persuades others to get involved. It conveys the urgency of the cause and inspires people to pick up a shovel and help out. Simply put, you cannot light a fire under other people if you are not on fire yourself.

All of the successful social entrepreneurs I interviewed have a hearty charge of passion. As I mentioned in chapter 1, this passion comes from having seen or experienced the problem they are trying to solve firsthand: they have seen the squalor of poverty, they have experienced violence in their schools, they have been to children's hospitals, they have had illnesses in their families. After witnessing an enormous need, they have developed compassion for the sufferers, then jumped in with incredible zeal for the cause. As the leader of a new organization, you need to help other people experience this same process; if you don't, you will never attract enthusiastic participants. People need to see the problem up close, develop their own passion, and decide to take action. It's up to you to help them "see it, feel it, do it!"

I learned the power of this principle when I volunteered to help build a new park in our city. It is located on a hill that overlooks the entire valley. Over 150 years ago, the founders of the city climbed this hill and laid out the roads and significant sites before doing any building. New homes were starting to encroach on the hill, and we were losing a significant part of our history. In our first meeting, we created a lengthy list of prominent people we thought might help. When we contacted these people, every one of them said, "Sorry, I'm already involved in other causes." We struck out completely! We soon learned that we needed to take people to the actual site to get them excited. They had to climb the hill and see the breathtaking view, hear the history of the city, see the encroaching homes, and visualize the sixty-six-acre park, which included hiking trails, plaques, and a monument. Everyone we got up on the hill was willing to donate money, labor, or services. In time, we recruited an army of supporters and finished the park.

So having the passion yourself is not enough. You have to be able to effectively convey it to others. I once met a woman who loved a certain author and promoted his cause. Then she heard him speak in person; he was overweight, poorly dressed, and rather mundane—her enthusiasm waned significantly. A year later she heard him again; he was trim, well dressed, and extremely dynamic—so she got back on board. The rumor was that he had hired a public-speaking consultant to help him improve his presentation. At the time, I thought it was humorous that this woman was so affected by this man's appearance and delivery. I now realize that the only thing people have to bet on initially is you, the founder of the organization. I'm not suggesting extensive attempts at image management, but you have to be able to infectiously pass your passion on to others.

In sum, the first step is to make sure you possess the passion yourself. Do you want to start this organization more than anything else? Is it what you really want to achieve in life? Are you willing to sacrifice time and conveniences to make it happen? If you cannot answer yes to these questions, you won't have staying power. The next step is to make sure you can effectively proclaim your cause to others. You are the standard bearer for your organization and need to tell the story over and over again. And you need to do it in a succinct and persuasive manner. So refine your message, polish your presentational skills, and be prepared to show people the problem firsthand so they can develop their own zeal for the cause. If you have the passion yourself but cannot effectively communicate it, your new venture will never get off the ground. The principle is this: Possess it, proclaim it!

KEY 2: KEEP YOUR FOCUS

An important part of proclaiming your passion is having a crystal-clear focus. No organization can be everything to everyone. Effective organizations create a clear statement of purpose that lets people know what they are and what they are not. A well-crafted mission statement drives all the activities of the organization—it is the foundation for goals, programs, and decision-making.

In the for-profit world, organizations change their focus from time to time based on new technology and changing customer preferences. In fact, our best entrepreneurs constantly scramble after new opportunities, abandon products and services that no longer work, and shift their resources to more fruitful areas. One of my favorite entrepreneurial heroes is June Morris, the founder of Morris Travel and Morris Air. Over a period of time, June transformed her organization from a travel agency to a leisure travel business to a charter travel company to a full-fledged airline—which she sold to Southwest Airlines for $139 million. Although her focus was very clear while cultivating each venture, her focus changed as more promising opportunities presented themselves.

Unfortunately, our toughest social problems remain fairly constant. The challenges of hunger, poverty, and various illnesses do not change as briskly as consumer needs and preferences. These problems are fairly entrenched and take a long time to dislodge. Consequently, social entrepreneurs need a constant focus over a long period of time—at least until the problem is resolved or significantly reduced. That does not mean you don't have to innovate new technology, training programs, or delivery systems relative to the problem. But if you attack hunger one year, poverty the next, and illiteracy after that, you won't solve anything. As Nancy Brinker suggests, "focus, focus, focus, and more focus" is critical to building a successful nonprofit organization.

The best mission statements create a compelling vision of the future. Martin Luther King is a great example of a leader who captured people's hearts with his vision. In his famous "I Have a Dream" speech, he didn't say, "It would be nice if we could work together." He said, "I have a dream" and then went on to portray a new America where blacks and whites work together in the spirit of brotherhood, making judgments based on character, not skin color. Wernher von Braun, the head of NASA during the '60s, is another great leader who took people's hearts by storm. His mission: To put a man on the moon by the end of the decade. This objective drove everything NASA did during this period. On July 20, 1969, Neil Armstrong and Edwin Aldrin became the first human beings to walk upon the moon. If von Braun's mission had been "to advance space travel," he might not have been so successful.

The social entrepreneurs in this book all have clear and inspiring missions. Peter Gold wants disadvantaged children in America to have their own first book. Nancy Brinker wants to eradicate breast cancer. Aubyn Burnside wants children in foster care to have their own suitcases. Rita Ungaro-Schiavone wants elderly shut-ins to enjoy seven healthy meals each week. And Henri Landwirth is making sure no more children die in America before their last wish is fulfilled.

An important part of keeping your focus in the nonprofit world is not duplicating what another organization is already doing well. In the for-profit arena, many companies create "me too" products and compete head-to-head with other businesses. Our best entrepreneurs, however, find unique needs no one else is meeting, then pursue them to the fullest. This strategy is also critical for community-service organizations. Remember, you are trying to solve a serious social problem, not become a legend yourself. If someone else is already doing a pretty good job addressing the issue, join forces with them—use your passion and skills to make their organization better. If you end up competing for patrons to serve, limited resources, and volunteers, your organization will sputter and die.

The social entrepreneurs I interviewed have done an excellent job meeting unique needs no one else is addressing. Rather than compete with existing hunger organizations, Paulette Hardin and her friends at SHARE help people stretch their food dollar. Stedman Graham has created the drug-education program for schools and existing community organizations. Peter Gold supports dozens of literacy programs rather than compete with them. And Patience White has gained great support for her organization because she doesn't duplicate existing government services. So develop a crystal-clear focus, different from that of other organizations, and plan on staying with it for a long time.

KEY 3: WORK WITH TENACITY

No quality appears more often in my interviews with entrepreneurs than raw tenacity. And it is absolutely critical to getting a new organization off the ground! Tenacity is much more than just hard work. It is holding on with a firm grasp, plowing forward in spite of unfavorable odds, and never giving up. All successful entrepreneurs have numerous chances to quit along the way, but they don't. They work exhausting hours, do much of the work themselves, and hang in there long enough to triumph. Part of it comes from their passion. Another part comes from a strong belief in personal control: these people take full responsibility for their lives, their organizations, and the outcomes of their actions. When things don't go right, they don't blame someone else; instead, they figure out how to turn things around. This attitude empowers them to act courageously, alter their approach, and relentlessly persist.

As with passion and focus, tenacity is even more critical in the nonprofit world. For-profit entrepreneurs can persuade people with a variety of incentives: "The salary is great." "The return on your investment will be strong." "There are lots of opportunities for advancement in our company." Social entrepreneurs have to appeal to people's hearts: "These children need our help." "We are saving lives." "You can help us relieve this suffering." This type of persuasion always take longer and requires more patience. Rather than bailing out when things get tough—which many people do in this kind of work—successful social entrepreneurs hang in there long enough to make their organizations survive, then thrive. They become highly skilled at getting over mountains, under hurdles, and around roadblocks.

Bob Macauley is a tenacious hero in the nonprofit world. He is the founder of AmeriCares, an organization that provides relief to people in foreign lands following serious disaster. Bob simply won't take no for an answer when he's trying to save lives. He's not afraid to call presidents, kings, and queens to see if they will help. Over the years, AmeriCares has provided millions of dollars in medicines and supplies to the desperately needy in more than fifty countries—often within hours after disaster strikes. When the devastating earthquake hit Armenia, Bob had a plane full of supplies en route before landing permits had even been obtained. The pilot called from Canada—still no permits. He called from Belgrade—still no permits. Bob finally secured the necessary permits well beyond the point of no return in Russian territory. Bob's philosophy: "If you are going to do something, someone will always present you with nine reasons why it can't be done. Just mow 'em all down. Make things happen."

While Bob Macauley has figured out how to provide rapid relief to disaster victims, most social entrepreneurs work on problems that are deeply ingrained in society. Hunger, poverty, illiteracy, violence, and various illnesses can take years and even decades to resolve. If you work on one of those challenges, you'll need a hearty dose of tenacity for years. If you aren't realistic about what is required, you'll end up disliking your work. Volunteers will fall through, corporate sponsors will back out, and roadblocks will arise that you didn't plan on facing. As this happens over and over, what started off as a passionate cause can become a ball and chain around your leg. So expectations can make or break your new venture. Many nonprofit organizations have failed because the founders thought the problem they were addressing would be easier and quicker to solve.

In sum, plan on being married to your mission, especially during the start-up years: you'll eat it, drink it, breathe it, and sleep it. And sometimes you'll fret about it during long restless nights. Recall how many of the entrepreneurs in this book have worked tenaciously for years to be where they are today. So if you aren't brimming with passion, don't like the weight of responsibility, and aren't willing to work day and night with Macauley-like tenacity, you probably don't have the stomach for social entrepreneuring. You'd be better off paying your dues for membership in America by volunteering in someone else's organization—which is also a great thing to do! You don't have to start a nonprofit venture to make a major contribution in this country. Everyone should contribute at whatever level he or she can.

KEY 4: BUILD THE RIGHT TEAM

Successful entrepreneurs thrive on the experience of others. They understand their limitations and enlist people to fill in the gaps. They not only have a real knack for finding partners with compensating talents, but they are also able to "lock in" people with passion for the venture and enthusiasm for teamwork. Indeed, they are master puzzle makers who quickly put all the pieces in place. Recruiting strong team members early is critical to getting new ventures over the rocky road of entrepreneuring. In today's breakneck business environment, there just isn't time to muddle along alone. Aspiring entrepreneurs who try to do everything themselves usually fail.

The team is everything in community-service organizations. The whole is indeed greater than the sum of its parts. You get a lot more from a group of passionate citizens solving problems together than you ever could from individuals working alone. The experience base is greater, perspectives are broader, solutions are better, and confidence is enhanced when community members unite in a common cause.

When building your team, make sure all of the bases are covered. Inventory your own strengths and weaknesses and match them up with the requirements of your mission. Since no individual ever has all the talent required, you will need to find people to fill in the skills and experience you are lacking. Start by making a "wish list" of the people you hope to enlist. First, identify people with technical know-how relevant to your cause. For example, if you are working on a particular health issue, you will need medical specialists in that area. Second, identify people with contacts in the field. If you plan to implement your program through the religious community, you will need members of the clergy on your team. Finally, identify people with business and organizational skills. The more bases you cover here, the better: strategy, legal, finance, public relations, and operations.

Once you identify potential team members, choose the ones with the most passion for your cause. Part of igniting their enthusiasm is up to you. Help them see and understand the problem and feel compassion for the sufferers. In the end, you are always better off to select people with incredible zeal and adequate skills than people with worlds of talent but no passion for your mission—such people probably won't join your team anyway.

In addition to passion, you need the right personalities on your team. Fortunately, we have decades of research and practical experience to guide us here. Ideal team members enjoy working in groups, believe everyone has something to contribute, respect other people's positions, and don't crave personal credit. Most important, they check their egos at the door and work toward a team consciousness. People who need to be in charge, think they are smarter than everybody else, and hog all the credit just don't make good team members. As with passion, it's better to choose people with adequate talent and enthusiasm for teamwork than superstars with anti-team personalities.

You can organize your team members in a number of ways depending on the size of your organization and the scope of your mission. It helps to have a few highly committed people to share the day-to-day operation of the organization. These people should have the same passion and tenacity you do. Recall how Mick Shannon partnered up with Joe Lake, Peter Gold worked with Kyle Zimmer, and Tammy Bird received great support from Melinda McMullen. Next, you need a strong board of directors. This is your decision-making body, so all the technical and business bases need to be covered within this group. Finally, having a board of advisers is a great idea for most nonprofit organizations. These people are less involved in day-to-day operations, but they have valuable skills and experience to contribute. They might be technical experts, people with contacts, or corporate partners. Because social problems are complex, the broader the representation, the better. This not only leads to better solutions, it also enhances commitment in the community for your cause.

The social entrepreneurs in this book are wonderful team builders. Much of their success is a function of the dynamic teams they have built. Meredith Blake of Break the Cycle is a superb example. Though trained in the law, she recognized her limitations in other aspects of domestic violence. From the beginning, she concentrated on building relationships with people who could help. Each time she met with someone, she asked for three additional names. In each meeting she said, "I have no materials, staff, or office space. If you join me, you'll really need to roll up your sleeves and work." While this scared some people off, it helped Meredith find a core group of passionate and committed partners. In addition to recruiting a strong board, she immediately established a cross-disciplinary advisory committee of teachers, doctors, social workers, and lawyers. She now has dozens of talented professionals working in her organization. Much of Break the Cycle's success is a result of Meredith's powerful team.

Picking the right team members is one of the most important things you will do in social entrepreneuring. I've seen nonprofit organizations full of passionate people who lack technical and business skills. I've also seen teams of talented folks who lack passion and perseverance. Both types of organizations struggle to achieve their objectives. The time you spend enlisting people with the right skills, passion, and personalities will pay off tenfold in achieving the mission of your organization. So pick your team wisely!

KEY 5: LEAVE YOUR EGO BEHIND

For-profit entrepreneurs start organizations for a variety of reasons: independence, freedom, wealth, power, prestige. None of these is the right reason for starting a nonprofit organization. The overarching objective in service work has to be improving the lives of the people you are serving. This objective is more important than anything else, including you as the founder of the organization. If the focus is on you, you will mislead your team.

Kahlil Gibran, the renowned Lebanese poet, once wrote, "A root is a flower that disdains fame." This metaphor describes the attitude of our top social entrepreneurs—they build strong teams, get their systems operating, then step into the background to sustain the organization. In chapter 1, I mentioned the Human Service Alliance in Winston-Salem, North Carolina. The founders of this remarkable organization are so far in the background you can't even find them. I called HSA several times hoping to arrange an interview with one of the founders—no one would even tell me who they are: "Just a group of compassionate citizens who want to provide selfless service to the terminally ill." Selfless service describes their philosophy well. It means the "self" is not in it. It is service for its own sake. It is kindness without strings attached. It is giving with no expectation of reward or recognition. It is an outward expression of unconditional love.

The entrepreneurs in this book are exceptional examples of *selfless* service. They remain focused on their mission, not on themselves. At the Children's Miracle Network, the kids always come first. It doesn't matter if you are a movie star, a famous athlete, or the president of a major corporation; you take a back seat to the children being served. At Casa Linda, Linda Kantor stepped back to make sure the organization would continue beyond her. When people take visitors on tours around the center, they never talk about Linda. What they say is, "*We* did this" or "This is *our* program." At Food From the 'Hood, everything Tammy Bird does is for the students at Crenshaw High School. She is seldom mentioned in any of the literature prepared by the organization. It's about the students, not about Tammy.

In his influential book *Half Time,* Bob Buford discusses the shift from success to significance many of us make in our lives. During the first part of our careers, we are preoccupied with ourselves: our schooling, our grades, our first job, our salary, our promotions, our recognition, and so on. We are like a spring winding tighter and tighter on itself. At some point, we take a halftime break to think about the rest of our lives. Many of us make the decision to stop chasing success and start pursuing significance. As our focus shifts from self to others, we are like a spring unwinding outward, away from the center. Giving up our tightly wound self to participate in something bigger is an immensely liberating experience. It helps us discover who we are and what we have to offer society.

For people raised in corporate America, leaving the ego behind is often difficult. According to Gandhi, "Many could forgo heavy meals, a full wardrobe, a fine house, et cetera; it is the ego they cannot forgo." But it can be done! When I started serving in the community, I had to remind myself, "This is not about you, Mike." Over time it got easier as I witnessed the results this attitude produces. When you serve others *selflessly,* magical things start to happen. You don't have to jockey for position, tilt the table in your favor, or camouflage hidden agendas. You don't have to be right all the time, so your mind is open to many unique viewpoints. You aren't threatened by people who are smarter or more skilled than you; in fact, you recruit them and celebrate their arrival. And if someone comes along who is more qualified to grow the organization than you are, that's okay too. Decisions are always better when the people you are serving come first, not you. If you truly are in it for sick children, troubled teenagers, or people living in poverty, your organization has a great chance of succeeding. So remember: It's not about you!

KEY 6: CREATE A LOW-COST SYSTEM

Effectiveness is achieving your goals; efficiency is doing it with as few resources as possible. Successful entrepreneurs are masters of efficiency. They are able to create something from practically nothing, get more from less along the way, and keep their costs below industry standards. They also learn to use an abundance of resources other than money to solve their problems. This keen eye for efficiency has enormous competitive advantages. It results in lower costs, superior products, better prices, and finer service than other companies can offer.

Efficiency is even more critical in the nonprofit arena. The last thing you want to do is create a high-cost structure that consumes valuable resources. When this happens, your focus shifts from serving your people to maintaining your system. If you get creative, you can always find ways to achieve your goals with lower costs. Here's an analogy I like to use: Suppose a bee is buzzing around your house—your goal is to get rid of it. One approach is to get a sledgehammer and start swinging; another is to use a fly swatter; a third is to simply open the door. All three strategies get rid of the bee, but they range from costly to efficient: the sledgehammer will damage the walls, the fly swatter is standard procedure, and opening the door is the most efficient.

Successful social entrepreneurs not only learn to open doors, but they also outlaw sledgehammers in their organizations. In other words, they achieve their objectives with as little cost as possible and refuse to adopt practices that consume valuable resources. We can learn a lot from their examples. Here are four strategies for setting up a low-cost system.

First, decentralize your efforts to spread your costs around. The idea is to create hundreds of satellite groups at the grassroots level as opposed to one costly central structure. While each group will have some costs to bear, no one entity will have to carry the full burden of the mission. This is what Joseph Grassi does with Skip-A-Meal: he teaches independent groups within the religious community how to run their own programs. Likewise, Aubyn Burnside helps numerous groups organize Suitcases For Kids in their own cities. Christmas in April has also expanded by adding affiliates across the country. In many cases, a local corporation donates an employee to head up the program in that city each year, which is an extremely efficient way to serve elderly and handicapped homeowners. Empowering passionate people at the local level not only spreads the costs around, but it also enhances commitment to the program in each community.

Second, learn to recycle constantly. Office-supply companies, furniture stores, various manufacturers, consignment shops, and restaurants all regularly dispose of surplus goods. The trick is to get these items before they end up in the dump. Rather than go out begging each time you need something, establish permanent relationships with companies that frequently replace or dispose of items you need. For example, the race of technology is so swift that many companies upgrade their information systems annually. By linking up with such a company, you can automatically get computers, printers, and phones every year. True, this equipment will be a bit dated, but you are solving a social problem, not chasing state-of-the-art competitors. You don't need the fanciest office furniture, computers, or filing cabinets. The advantage of getting these items for free far outweighs the disadvantage of having slightly used equipment. In addition, airlines and hotels often donate unused inventory to worthy causes. Link up with some of these companies, as Mick Shannon and Joe Lake did.

Third, co-opt permanent volunteers. Having to recruit people every time you need help is just as frustrating as constantly looking for money—it gets old fast. You can solve this problem by linking up with organizations that will provide volunteers on an ongoing basis. Pedro Greer, for example, created a course in homeless education at the University of Miami's medical school. Students in the program work at the Camillus Health Concern as part of their training, which has permanently solved Pedro's volunteer problem. Henri Landwirth has done the same thing by linking up with Disney and other corporate partners. All the volunteers needed by Give Kids the World are readily available. By far the best way to solve your volunteer problem is to have the recipients of your services work in the program. At Food From the 'Hood, the students work in the garden. At Delancey Street, the residents teach the classes and run the businesses. At SHARE, people who receive the groceries donate two hours each month to provide the distribution. These organizations have more volunteers than they can use.

Fourth, grow your organization through existing infrastructures. There is no reason to take on additional costs or marry bricks and mortar when existing organizations would welcome your program or services. Recall how Break the Cycle and Athletes Against Drugs are expanding through schools and other community organizations. Rather than reinventing the wheel, First Book is growing through existing literacy programs. And Aid For Friends is expanding through hundreds of churches and synagogues. Partnering up with organizations that share your cause is the quickest and most efficient way to expand your organization.

In sum, the nonprofit world is about problem-solving, not empire-building. To succeed, you must be incredibly efficient. There are always ways to make things happen without money, so don't institutionalize practices that drain your resources. Instead, decentralize your efforts and spread your costs around, learn to constantly recycle, co-opt permanent volunteers, and grow through existing infrastructures.

KEY 7: GENERATE YOUR OWN REVENUE

Many compassionate souls start nonprofit organizations to do something meaningful as opposed to something greedy. They may even bristle at such terms as *business, marketing,* and *profit.* Because their cause is good, they assume that people will appear with contributions and everything will work out. This attitude initiates an ongoing cycle of begging for whatever money is left over in America after individuals, families, and corporations pay their bills. Unfortunately, competition for this money is fierce, and chasing it is unpleasant. If you rely on others to give you money, your fate will always be in their hands. This not only makes planning and meeting objectives difficult, but it is also disheartening to have the future of a cause you believe in so strongly be outside your control.

The truth is, all organizations need revenue to accomplish their missions. If you don't have enough to cover your costs, you won't survive. If you barely cover your costs, you'll limp along. If you cover your costs and have money left over, you'll not only survive but you'll thrive. Surplus funds allow you to develop new products, enhance your programs, improve your services, and expand your enterprise. Successful social entrepreneurs understand that profit is the lifeblood of their organization. They are comfortable with it, they seek it, they create it. Generating your own revenue puts the destiny of your organization in your own hands.

There are several ways to generate revenue for your venture. The first is through partnerships with corporations. In my book *Glorious Accidents,* I discuss the tendency of America's top for-profit entrepreneurs to give back to their communities. These business founders are funding cancer research, feeding the poor, aiding the homeless, supporting schools, lowering grocery costs, rebuilding cathedrals, disseminating health information, and helping families of the chronically ill. As it turns out, charitable giving is a sound business strategy. When a business supports the community, the community supports that business. Charitable giving, however, is always secondary to the mission of for-profit ventures. If your organization can become the vehicle for meeting corporations' desire to give—so they can focus on their primary mission—you have a win-win situation.

Billy Shore is the master of partnering up with corporations. Reread his story in this book, and read his books *Revolution of the Heart* and *The Cathedral Within.* The concept is fairly simple. You figure out what you have to offer an organization, then join together to create new wealth neither of you could generate alone. Billy's relationship with Calphalon Cookware is a perfect example: Calphalon manufactures a two-quart sauté pan, Share Our Strength contributes its logo and chefs for cooking demonstrations, and pan sales go up. This new revenue benefits both organizations. Peter Gold has done the same thing with First Book. Businesses in the book industry support his organization, and he helps enhance their reputation and visibility in the community. Both groups win, which is what a true partnership is all about. Meredith Blake is also trying to do this at Break the Cycle. She has access to the young adult population, which is an attractive market to many organizations. With her savvy, I'm sure she'll put together a number of win-win partnerships.

In addition to partnering up with corporations, you can generate revenue through your own products and services. Mimi Silbert is a champion of this strategy. The people she serves—ex-convicts and drug addicts—help her create and run ventures that support Delancey Street. These businesses then provide career training for those in her program. In like manner, Bill Strickland has started a food-service company, a recording venture, and a real-estate business to support the Manchester Craftsmen's Guild. Tammy Bird and her students at Crenshaw High School have created a brand of salad dressing that supports Food From the 'Hood. Anthony Shriver has generated several million dollars for Best Buddies through his limited-edition art. Nancy Brinker has created an annual event, Race for the Cure, that raises millions of dollars for the Komen Breast Cancer Foundation. Of course, SHARE has the ultimate strategy. The organization receives ongoing revenue from the people it serves. Families pay $14 each month to get nearly $30 worth of groceries. As long as the organization continues to provide value, SHARE will never have to beg for money from anyone.

Obviously, your products and services have to be good. You can't sell junk and expect people to buy it just because it helps a worthy cause. But if you offer high-quality items at competitive prices, being part of a worthy cause can significantly increase your sales. So what do you have to offer that people will pay for? Is it an event like Race for the Cure? Is it a product line like salad dressing? Is it a moving company? Is it a consulting service? Time spent developing products and services will have a high payoff for your organization. Generating your own revenue is the path to independence and sustainability. Remember, *profit* is not a dirty word. It is the lifeblood of your organization!

KEY 8: APPLY BEST BUSINESS PRACTICES

The term *nonprofit* is misleading. It tells us what these organizations are not; it doesn't tell us what they are. If it isn't clear by now, nonprofit organizations are businesses. They involve mobilizing individuals and resources to meet needs in the community. They require strategy, finance, marketing, customer service, and compliance with the law. Founders of nonprofit ventures need the same management skills as founders of for-profit organizations. They may need more vision, passion, tenacity, and team-building talent. While the principles reviewed here have special relevance in the nonprofit sector, other concepts also apply.

This is not the place to review all the practices that make organizations great. But create a development plan for yourself and key members of your team. Read the latest books by our top management gurus: Peter Drucker, Gary Hamel, Rosabeth Moss Kanter, Michael Hammer, and others. Attend the best seminars on business strategy, public relations, and team-building. And make sure you cultivate entrepreneurship, which I believe is the leadership model of the future. In order to keep up with the demands of a growing nonprofit enterprise, you will need to constantly improve your skills.

In summary, the nonprofit sector will become increasingly important in future decades. If you learn to build and run community-service organizations, you will be extremely valuable to society. You'll have a wonderfully rewarding experience serving others; you'll make America a better place to live; you'll become one of our nation's new heroes. The future depends on what we do today; it's never too late to create the country we are capable of becoming. As Gandhi once said, "You must be the change you wish to see in the world." So gain business-management skills, apply the principles reviewed here, and learn from the exceptional role models in this book. This is your path to building a successful nonprofit organization.

Happy social entrepreneuring!

CONTACT INFORMATION

SERVING OUR CHILDREN

Give Kids the World
210 South Bass Road
Kissimmee, Florida 34746
(407) 396-1114

Suitcases For Kids
29 Seventh Avenue NE
Hickory, North Carolina 28601
(828) 328-3645

Children's Miracle Network
4525 South 2300 East, Suite 202
Salt Lake City, Utah 84117
(801) 278-8900

First Book
1319 F Street, N.W., Suite 500
Washington, D.C. 20004
(202) 393-1222

Camp Mak-A-Dream
P. O. Box 1450
Missoula, Montana 59806
(406) 549-5987

TEACHING OUR YOUTH

Food From the 'Hood
5010 11th Avenue
Los Angeles, California 90043
(888) 601-FOOD

Manchester Craftsmen's Guild
1815 Metropolitan Street
Pittsburgh, Pennsylvania 15233
(412) 322-1773

Athletes Against Drugs
455 N. CityFront Plaza, 15th Floor
Chicago, Illinois 60611
(312) 321-3400

Break the Cycle
P. O. Box 1797
Santa Monica, California 90406-1797
(310) 319-1339

The Heart of America
201 Massachusetts Avenue, NE, Suite C5
Washington, D.C. 20002
(202) 546-3256

HEALING OUR AFFLICTED

Camillus Health Concern
P. O. Box 012408
Miami, Florida 33101
(305) 374-1065

Susan G. Komen Breast Cancer Foundation
5005 LBJ Freeway, Suite 370
Dallas, Texas 75244
(972) 855-1600

Best Buddies International
100 S.E. 2nd Street, Suite 1990
Miami, Florida 33131
(305) 374-2233

Delancey Street Foundation
600 The Embarcadero
San Francisco, California 94107
(415) 957-9800

Adolescent Employment Readiness Center
Children's National Medical Center
111 Michigan Avenue, N.W., Suite 1303
Washington, D.C. 20010
(202) 884-3203

FEEDING OUR HUNGRY

Aid For Friends
2869 Holme Avenue
Philadelphia, Pennsylvania 19152-2118
(215) 464-2224

Bea Gaddy's Family Centers
P. O. Box 38501
Baltimore, Maryland 21231
(410) 563-2749

Share Our Strength
733 15th Street, N.W., Suite 640
Washington, D.C. 20005
(202) 393-2925

Skip-A-Meal
C/O Religious Studies Department
Santa Clara University
500 El Camino Real Boulevard
Santa Clara, California 95053

World SHARE
6950 Friars Road
San Diego, California 92108
(800) 266-2202

AIDING OUR NEEDY

The Redistribution Center
7736 Hoyt Circle
Arvada, Colorado 80005
(303) 431-0904

Community Hope Center
P. O. Box 124
Cottage Hills, Illinois 62018
(618) 259-0959

Christmas in April USA
1536 Sixteenth Street, NW
Washington, D.C. 20036-1402
(202) 483-9083

Cranks Creek Survival Center
P. O. Box 32
Cranks Creek, Kentucy 40820
(606) 573-2812

Casa Linda
135 Sylvan Avenue
New Haven, Connecticut 06519
(203) 773-1847

REFERENCES

CHAPTER 1: SERVICE AS A WAY OF LIFE IN AMERICA

Inc., Special Issue: The State of Small Business, May 1997.

Glauser, Michael J. *Glorious Accidents: How Everyday Americans Create Thriving Companies.* Salt Lake City: Shadow Mountain, 1998.

Wills, Garry. *Inventing America: Jefferson's Declaration of Independence.* New York: Doubleday & Company, 1978.

"Constitution of the United States." *World Book Encyclopedia, Volume 4.* Chicago: Scott Fetzer Company, 1989, 994–1,014.

De Tocqueville, Alexis. *Democracy in America: A New Translation by George Lawrence.* New York: Harper & Row, 1966.

Gross, James A., and Andre B. Collins. *Gettysburg: The Souvenir Guide to the National Military Park.* Gettysburg, Pennsylvania, 1991.

Chamberlain, Joshua Lawrence. *Through Blood and Fire at Gettysburg.* Gettysburg: Stan Clark Military Books, 1994.

Pullen, John J. *The Twentieth Maine: A Volunteer Regiment in the Civil War.* Dayton: Morningside House, 1997.

Wills, Garry. *Lincoln at Gettysburg.* New York: Touchstone, 1992.

Shore, Bill. *Revolution of the Heart.* New York: Riverhead Books, 1995.

Raynolds, John. *The Halo Effect: How Volunteering Can Lead to a More Fulfilling Life—and a Better Career.* New York: Golden Books, 1998.

"Melancholy Nation." *U.S. New & World Report.* March 8, 1999, 56–63.

Erickson, Milton H. *Teaching Seminar with Milton H. Erickson, M.D.* New York: Brunner/Mazel, 1980.

Kilpatrick, Joseph, and Sanford Danziger. *Better Than Money Can Buy.* Winston-Salem: Innersearch, 1996.

CHAPTER 2: SERVING OUR CHILDREN

"Population" and "Vital Statistics." *Statistical Abstract of the United States.* U.S. Bureau of the Census, 1998.

"U.S. Teenage Pregnancy Statistics." The Alan Guttmacher Institute, 1998. www.agi-usa.org/teen_preg/special_report.html

Statistics compiled by the National Center for Health Statistics, 1996. www.dhhs.gov/news/press/1996pres/960624b.html

Statistics compiled by World Hunger Year, 505 Eighth Avenue, 21st Floor, New York, New York 10018. www.worldhungeryear.org

Shore, Bill. *Revolution of the Heart.* New York: Riverhead Books, 1995.

Statistics compiled by The Children's Health Fund, 317 East 64th Street, New York, New York 10021. www.childrenshealth-fund.org

"Cancer Facts and Figures, 1997." Statistics compiled by the American Cancer Society. www.cancer.org/statistics/97/cff/97chidr.html

CHAPTER 3: TEACHING OUR YOUTH

Niehoff, Debra. *The Biology of Violence: How Understanding the Brain, Behavior, and Environment Can Break the Vicious Cycle of Aggression.* New York: Free Press, 1999.

"Massacre in Colorado." *Newsweek,* Special Report, May 3, 1999, 22–39.

Shore, Bill. *Revolution of the Heart.* New York: Riverhead Books, 1995.

"Law Enforcement, Courts, and Prisons." *Statistical Abstract of the United States.* U.S. Bureau of the Census, 1998.

"Street Gang Dynamics." Statistics compiled by The Nawojczyk Group, P. O. Box 1932, North Little Rock, Arkansas 72115. www.gangwar.com/dynamics.htm

CHAPTER 4: HEALING OUR
AFFLICTED

"Health and Nutrition." *Statistical Abstract of the United States.* U.S. Bureau of the Census, 1998.

"Alcoholism and Alcohol-Related Problems: A Sobering Look." Statistics compiled by the National Council on Alcoholism and Drug Dependence, 12 West 21st Street, New York, New York 10010. www.ncadd.org/problems.html

"Mental Illness Statistics." Statistics compiled by Ryan Robbins. www.geocities.com/TheTropics/1538/stats.html

"Facts about Mental Retardation." Statistics compiled by Best Buddies International, 100 SE Second Street, Suite 1990, Miami, Florida 33131.

Statistics compiled by the Susan G. Komen Breast Cancer Foundation, 5005 LBJ Freeway, Suite 370, Dallas, Texas 75244. www.breastcancerinfo.com

Statistics compiled by the Adolescent Employment Readiness Center, Children's National Medical Center, 111 Michigan Avenue N.W., Washington, D.C. 20010.

CHAPTER 5: FEEDING OUR HUNGRY

"Hunger in America." Statistics compiled by MAZON. www.shamash.org/soc- action/mazon/mazon_hunger.html

Statistics compiled by World Hunger Year, 505 Eighth Avenue, 21st Floor, New York, New York 10018. www.worldhungeryear.org

Shore, Bill. *Revolution of the Heart.* New York: Riverhead Books, 1995.

"USDA Food Recovery and Gleaning Initiative." USDA, 3101 Park Center Drive, Room 819, Alexandria, Virginia 22302. www.usda.gov/fcs/glean.htm

CHAPTER 6: AIDING OUR NEEDY

Statistics compiled by World Hunger Year, 505 Eighth Avenue, 21st Floor, New York, New York 10018. www.worldhungeryear.org

"Why Are People Homeless?" Statistics compiled by the National Coalition for the Homeless, 1012 Fourteenth Street, N.W., Suite 600, Washington, D.C. 20005. http://nch.ari.net/causes.html.

"Homelessness and Poverty in America." Statistics compiled by the National Law Center On Homelessness and Poverty, 918 F Street, N.W., Suite 412, Washington, D.C. 20004. www.nlchp.org/contact.htm.

"Income, Expenditures, and Wealth." *Statistical Abstract of the United States.* U.S. Bureau of the Census, 1998.

CHAPTER 7: BUILDING A SUCCESSFUL NONPROFIT ORGANIZATION

Glauser, Michael J. *Glorious Accidents: How Everyday Americans Create Thriving Companies.* Salt Lake City: Shadow Mountain, 1998.

Halamandaris, William. *Profiles in Caring: The Most Caring People in America.* Washington, D.C.: Caring Publishing, 1991, 125–28.

Kilpatrick, Joseph, and Sanford Danziger. *Better Than Money Can Buy.* Winston-Salem: Innersearch, 1996.

Buford, Bob. *Half Time: Changing Your Game Plan from Success to Significance.* Grand Rapids: Zondervan Publishing House, 1994.

Shore, Bill. *Revolution of the Heart.* New York: Riverhead Books, 1995.

Shore, Bill. *The Cathedral Within: Transforming Your Life By Giving Something Back.* New York: Random House, 1999.

INDEX